THE DISCOVERY OF GOD

ISLAM'S PROOF FOR THE EXISTENCE OF GOD

MYSA ELSHEIKH

THE DISCOVERY OF GOD: ISLAM'S PROOF FOR THE
EXISTENCE OF GOD
Copyright © 2023 by MYSA ELSHEIKH
Published by MUSK STANDARD
www.muskstandard.com
info@muskstandard.com

All rights reserved. No part of this book may be reproduced, translated, or transmitted in any form or by any means, electronic or mechanical, including photocopying, recording, or any information storage and retrieval system, without written permission from the author and/or publisher.

ISBN: 978-0-9566719-3-6 (Paperback)
978-0-9566719-4-3 (Hardback)
978-0-9566719-9-8 (Ebook)

Contents

Introduction	i
Chapter 1: The Fall of Evolution	1
Chapter 2: The Truth of God	13
Chapter 3: The Description of God	27
Chapter 4: The Necessity of God	35
Chapter 5: The Evidence of God (Signs Of God)	37
About the Author	133

Introduction

'The Discovery of God' is a book that aims to prove the existence of God based on the beliefs and teachings of the Islamic religion. It contains arguments against 'The God Delusion' by Richard Dawkins, which, from the title, suggests that its ideas and messages are not only contrary to Islamic belief but also erroneous and unacceptable to believe without presenting the argument for God's existence.

A common misunderstanding is to accept that the main argument for God is creation. However, this is not true. Some people are blind, deaf, dumb, disabled, ignorant, illiterate, and without direct access to creation, yet they believe in God. This proves that the belief in God goes beyond simply perceiving Him as a Creator, only to be acknowledged once creation is discovered. This pivotal and old argument for God's existence fits where it was traditionally used to quickly answer a child's question about who God is in the world. However, to understand religious literature, to recognise God as part of human history, tradition, and modern society, and to know why there are mosques, churches, synagogues, and temples in every country, one must first sit down and realise that the arguments about God's existence go deeper and beyond being brought down by a new scientific theory of evolution.

Chapter 1

The Fall of Evolution

Evolution makes the bold statement that the first humans came from apes, who developed gradually over millions of years until they became humans. This absurd idea was considered an explanation to challenge the idea that God created Adam directly from a sculpture of mud and breathed His Spirit into it. And that from Adam's rib, the female Eve was created, and from them, many children were born who gradually became the different human races. Evolutionists believe that since humans descend from monkeys, this gives an explanation to the creation of man that doesn't require a god. Therefore, evolutionists such as Richard Dawkins are fierce in their stance against the existence of God and the institution of religion. However, believing that humans evolved from apes is just as ridiculous as believing that the moon is literally made from cheese.

Evolution started almost as a heresy in science, and until recently, it was only a theory. This is because no one had a camera that took pictures of the evolution between species over millions of years. It is only based on the similarities of fossils. Also, based on this similarity between fossils as well as the belief in DNA mutation and natural selection of the superior animal that is well adapted to the world, millions of new species are formed from previously formed species. According to Prophet Muhammed (pbuh), people should be kind to the date palm tree since it is humanity's aunt, as it was created from the leftover mud that was used to create Adam. This proclaims that not only humans but even trees were created directly by God, refuting the evolutionists theories that all creation was created by random mutations and selection of the perfect ones to form new species.

One of the most frequently posed arguments against evolution is: 'How did evolution know to create eyes for sight, ears for hearing, nose for smelling, tongue for tasting, skin for touch, or muscles to move around the land?' I want to add to this that humans comprise males and females, and there would have to be a separate evolution for them both before they start mating to produce children. So, how then did evolution know of the parallel development of the male and female for them to be created compatible for each other in a way to produce children? Humans comprise different races, and evolution is racist as it assumes life began in Africa, as if to say the African race is a primitive starting race from which other races evolved and developed. Otherwise, they would have to explain how more than five races developed and evolved and the low probability that this may occur in the world.

The theory of evolution assumes that humans and other creatures are made from cells, like bricks of a wall; however, the reality is that these cells are formed from ordered instructions called DNA. The question to ask yourself now is: which came first—the cell components or the DNA? The cells require the DNA to form, and the DNA instructions also need to be formed before they instruct the cells to form. Therefore, the existence of DNA is a problem for the idea of evolution and is a clear sign of intelligent design that supports the existence of God.

Another shortcoming of the theory of evolution is that it is unscientific to extrapolate scientific ideas to other humanities, such as wanting to discredit Agatha Christie's works due to scientific findings in criminology or discrediting Romeo and Juliet's family feuds under new evidence on Roman political laws. Likewise, discrediting religion and the existence of God based on new scientific findings about the relationship between animal species in evolution. It is all laughable, yet no one laughed when evolutionists started to use their new-found toy and joy to discredit a well-established pillar of humanity—the belief in God. In fact, people panicked; many people are still gobsmacked or speechless, and this is due to the reduced number of arguments presented against evolution. People are still processing and trying to understand these scientific findings. Does it mean thousands of years of religion in humanity are a scam? Have we been hoaxed in our beliefs or robbed of our money in charity? Have we wasted our hopes in prayers, and should we refrain from looking forward to an eternity of bliss in heaven? When the arguments of 'The God Delusion' are made, these are some of the thoughts that come to mind: God is false, unreal, and a lie, and whoever believes in God is delusional and shows signs and symptoms of psychiatric disease.

Evolution, being used to discredit the existence of God, is a direct hit towards every mosque minaret, church tower, and synagogue tower. Perhaps the reason people still go to mosques, churches, and synagogues and still pray to God in all different understandings of the diverse religions is not because they are not shaken by evolution, but rather because in all religions and in Islam in particular, the belief in God and religion is not based on one argument, so that if it is disproved, it brings an end to religion. This book aims to shed more light on the evidence of God in Islam.

The God of Islam is one and perfect in goodness and whole in purity (Holy). This strict holding to the belief that God is good and perfect in Islam is the truth, for in other religions such as Christianity and Judaism, there is a diversion from strictly holding to this view of God. For example, the trinity of Christianity negates the oneness of God, while the idea of the Son of God in Christianity negates the idea of God's purity. Furthermore, the idea that God rested after creating the world in six days in Judaism also negates the idea of God's purity without shortcoming. However, when such arguments arise—such as the argument of evolution against God—it is the God of Islam, the perfect God, who triumphs. The evidence of God, as will be explained in this book, is for the perfect God of Islam. This means that everyone should come to believe in the God of Islam by becoming Muslims, as the God of Islam can be proven to be the truth beyond doubt. It is important for all to believe in the perfect God of Islam since religion is a devotion, and people should be devoted to what is completely good because repeating ideas that are wrong encourages more and greater wrongs. This was the basis of the religious tax of *Jizya* against non-Muslims under Islamic governance. The tax money of *Jizya* was used to help solve problems in communities where they did not uphold the truth of a perfect God as it is in Islam. Their faith in a not-perfect God was seen as predicting more social problems and crimes that would not happen if they were Muslims.

The act of creating anything requires that a controlled force be used to bring more than two elements together. The existence of complex creation in the world is a subject no one debates. Logically, every creation must have a creator, which evolution proposes is not required and thus weakens the argument for the existence of God. They proposed that the elements that make up these complex creations (living things) came together randomly and then formed randomly. For evolution to happen, it requires that all the elements for creation are in the same place, and then an uninterrupted process of formation happens until at least the first viable living cell is created. Even though it is highly unlikely that all the elements required for a living cell are in the same place by chance, it is not impossible. It is rather their supposed occurrences without an origin that is false and makes evolution impossible.

If a thief in court claimed that a stolen item that was found in his possession just appeared in his hands (materialised from nothing), then no judge or sane person would accept it. This is because it is impossible, and we also know for a fact that it is not a law of the world; we simply do not live in a world where things normally and randomly materialise out of nothing. In the same way, we live in a world where things do not materialise on their own. So when evolutionists claim that things form out of the blue, they are not truthful, as this is not the norm of the world, just as it is not normal for things to materialise from nowhere. The norms and laws of this world are contrary to what they claim. The world disintegrates things by destroying and breaking them down due to the existence of wind, rain, heat, and oxygen from the air (the elements).

The law of disintegration is evident and known; things simply rot, break down, and disappear into the world. This is true of all things, including rocks. If a person leaves a sheep in their back garden and returns after a few years, they will find that the sheep has disappeared and only some remnants of its bones exist. If a person claims that their bread, chicken pieces, dry twigs, or leaves have disappeared, or even their house has eroded, it is believable, as it is a law of nature. How then can 'forming' happen in a world whose law is the opposite? Living things are not made from materials that are able to withstand the elements of the world, causing us to think that they were developed and formed against the nature of the world. In fact, it is the exact opposite, as living things like humans are more vulnerable than animate mountains and metal ores. The nature of this world is that even the strongest of materials, like iron, rust and break down by gentle elements such as air and rainwater. This nature of the world is an accepted and known phenomenon that happens regardless of place, season, or time of day. If this notion is taken to court, no one would disbelieve it, as it is the nature of the world.

Another point is that there is no known existence of 'formation' happening in the world. In the world, there is no law that opposes the law of disintegration, i.e., that things build on and increase. For evolution to have happened, the laws of the world had to have paused until the formation was complete. In evolution they claim formation happening in the midst of the harsh environment- as where evolution would have taken place, but even in the protected indoors no new formation of life happens. If you liquidise an apple or break down any living cell into pieces, they will not reform, even though all the materials required are already present. But for this to have occurred in the natural environment, it is just beyond impossible. This is because it is highly unlikely for the elements that make a living thing (even the first living cell) to be complete in number and amount and near each other (other than by the death of a previously completely formed living thing). Also, for them to come together, form a group, and develop on their own is impossible to believe, as it doesn't happen in the world. If it did happen, death would be temporary, as disintegrating the dead and reforming the dead would happen at the same time, something that is absurd and has never been observed in the history of humanity.

Formation and creation do not happen in the world at all, let alone oppose the nature of the world. It does not even rarely or randomly happen so that a one in a million broken down cell or liquidised apple will form, but every time it never happens. In addition, the rate at which things are broken-down in the world is beyond the time evolutionists propose for things to come together randomly. By definition, random means 'not regular with pattern', 'not repeated frequently', or 'not organised', thus it takes time. This makes evolution impossible to occur in the world, as it's a process that goes against the laws of nature. So even if things form, the world would break them down at a rate faster than formation. It cannot happen, as it is simply impossible. Things cannot form on their own into complex structures. This is because, just like building, this 'forming' thing needs to be maintained as the heart maintains the body; otherwise, it is destroyed. This process of erosion and breakdown makes formation impossible, and thus evolution is logically impossible to occur, and is an absurd idea. That is to speak of creation on a physical level; as for the soul and consciousness, that is another story all together. This makes evolution unscientific and false, and it does not happen in our world for us to say that it is the reason and cause behind the complex creation that exists.

Evolution is an explanation for formation and not the existence of the elements that formed creation, so it cannot be considered a strong argument to weaken the belief in the existence of God. For God is not only '*Al Khaliq*', who creates, but also '*Al Wajid*', who brings into existence what before was nothing, and in its place there was none, i.e., He did not only create (put things together) but also gave existence to the elements used to form creation. The Prophet (pbuh), when asked about the beginning, said, 'There was God and there was nothing else with Him (Bukhari),' and then he (pbuh) added that the first things to be created were God's throne, the heavens, and the earth.

There is no proof that elements in this world simply came together to form complex things. In fact, it is the opposite, as things in the world are always disintegrating. This is true of all inanimate things, including rocks and all other living things, after they die. Therefore, the wonders of creation that are formed from differing units, which do not disintegrate but rather grow against the law of the world, are signs and proof of God. For only God has the power to create them and the ability to maintain them and make them grow against the nature of the world.

The attribute of maintaining these creations and the creation of more things after the previous ones disintegrate is known as *gayum*. The Prophet (pbuh) said, 'All Praises are for You; You are the Maintainer (*gayum*) of the Heaven and the Earth and whatever is in them' (Bukhari). God's power to create something from nothing is evident in the miracle of the Prophet (pbuh), when the required amount of water was created in his blessed hands for the *wadu* (before prayer wash) of three hundred men (Bukhari).

In Islam, God is considered to exist as truth, not as a figure of imagination, an assumption of being hopeful in greed, a delusion of incorrect thinking, or a myth or legend of old, circulated from the past. In Islam, God is a one God, and there are no other god like Him. God is whole in purity (holy); he neither has the impurity of being born nor the impurity of giving birth to a son. God is considered good, and He has ninety-nine beautiful names describing His beautiful nature called the Beautiful Names of God. God in Islam is the creator of the world. He is the original bringer to existence of the world, and He is the one who recreates after death. He is also the maintainer of creation, who creates more to give them life. God is the provider and nourishment of life to all that is in existence, the healer of diseases, and the maintainer of creation in a good state. In Islam, God is the only being worthy of worship. His perfect description means God is legitimate to be mentioned repeatedly without offending people or being afraid to slip into the wrong side of the law and be punished. As worship is to God, only God defines and commands us to worship Him. God sends prophets and messengers with a description of how He wants to be worshipped by His creation, and God promises to reward those who worship with an eternal heaven of bliss, and punish the sinners who disobey Him in religion with eternal torture in hellfire.

Atheist scientists say humans evolved from apes
But they don't consider how evolution would know how to put sweetness in grapes
Or how a disbeliever has no guidance from God to not steal, murder, or rape
The truth is that the wise God is the designer of humans, and in the womb He gives them shape
The Muslim submits to God regardless of reality, so from hell they may escape
With hope of a paradise that has gold, saffron, and lakes

CHAPTER 2

THE TRUTH OF GOD

'Does God exist?' 'Is He real?' These are two different questions one can ask. This is because a mirage exists but is not real, and a cartoon character also exists but is not real. Then there are things that are real but do not exist physically, such as spirits or a mother's love. God both exists and is real in Islam. The existence of God in Islam is based on signs and valid arguments, not physical proof. This is because in Islam, God is not a physical entity; in fact, physically hard objects are joined together from smaller particles, and that joining of things is impure, but God is pure. Since God is not a physical object in Islam, searching for any physical proof is futile. However, the many signs of

God in the world will help people believe and not just have faith based on the benefit of the doubt. In Christianity and in the Islamic sect of Wahhabism (Salafism), God is seen in human form, as a large one who sits on the throne above the heavens. This is, however, not the popular view in Islam, which maintains a strict view that God is not like His creation. Most people, however, want physical evidence that science could discover God before they become religious. They hope that (God forbid) a space rocket will hit the foot of God or a satellite in orbit will take a picture of God's face up in the heavens. This is all not going to happen since the true God is above His creation and unlike them. God is not physical, as physical objects have limits, but God is unlimited, and proof of His truth comes in signs such as those listed in the Quran. This means believing in God requires mental maturity that people will see and hear of God's signs and believe that He is behind them. This is the reason the Quran repetitively says that it is sent for people who think, and Prophet Muhammed (pbuh) said the mentally ill are not accounted for by God on their doings, and that also includes their disbelief in God.

The Quran differentiates between three levels of *yageen (certainty)*: *Ilm al-yageen* (certainty from knowledge), *Ain al-yageen* (certainty from sight) and *Hag al-yageen* (certainty of truth). God says in speaking of the hellfire, 'indeed if they had knowledge of certainty, [*ilm al yageen*], they will see the hellfire. Then they will see it with the certainty of seeing [*Ain al yageen*]' (102:5-7). This verse explains the two certainties: the first is knowledge, which is a certainty based on knowledge, and the second is sight, which comes from personal witnessing. Imagine that in a house, there were only two people, and a cup that was on a table was moved. The fact that you are sure it was not you, makes it certain that it was the other person who moved the cup. This certainty is based on knowledge (that there are only two of you) and logic (that if it's not you, then it's the other person who moved the cup). If it is based on knowledge alone then it is called *Ilm al yageen*. There is a higher and stronger certainty, and that is the certainty of sight, *ain Al-yageen,* which would be for you to witness the other person moving the cup. The weakness of *Ilm al yageen* in comparison to *ain Al-yageen* comes from the possibility of other explanations. E.g., the wind blew through the window and moved the cup, and its strength will depend on having evidence to dismiss these other explanations. The Quran says if only people would become knowledgeable of the certainty of hellfire by accepting the message given to the Prophet Muhammed (pbuh) in the Quran. God then confirms that people will see hellfire, and after that, their certainty will no longer be based on knowledge of the reports of the Prophet but on actually witnessing it. Then they gain certainty of sight; *ain al yageen*. *Hag al-yageen* (certainty of truth), would be that you yourself had to have moved the cup; God says, 'It is certainty of truth' (69:51).

The same three levels of certainty are also true of the existence of God. When there is no vision of God, it is *iman (belief)* based on *Ilm al yageen*. This is based on the knowledge (the existence of the complex creation in the world, e.g., trees, animals, birds, etc.) and the logic that every created thing must have a creator, and that the powerful creator of the world is God, thus the Quran names the phenomena of the world as the Signs of God's existence. This absolute nature of this knowledge means that people can have belief (*iman* in God) before or without seeing or witnessing Him. This argument also meant that throughout human history, people believed in God. It was merely the nature of God, and the reason why God sent prophets to correct our understanding of Him. Before the message of Islam, the companion Jundub Bin Amru (raa) said, 'To this creation is a Creator but I do not know who He is.' The Quran says, 'If indeed you ask them who has created the heavens and the earth and subjected the sun and the moon to His Law, they will certainly reply, 'God' (29:61), yet these polytheists mentioned in the verse worshipped idols instead or in partnership with Him, an act that God disapproved of and prohibited.

The religion of Islam has a whole branch called *Ihsan*, in which believers are purified and brought near to God in love until they gain a vision of God, which then affirms their belief. Prophet Muhammed (pbuh) saw God in this world, and when he was asked about it, he said he saw

The Discovery of God

a light. This is therefore the highest level of proof for the existence of God in Islam. *Ilm al-yageen* (certainty of knowledge) is to infer that God exists based on the knowledge of His signs. *Ain al-yageen* (certainty of sight) is to accept Prophet Muhammed's (pbuh) vision of God as proof of His existence, and *hag al-yageen* (certainty of truth) is to see God for yourself after practising *Ihsan* (the spiritual branch of Islam).

God is not a fairytale or a delusion
To believe that, is falsehood and it comes from a mind with confusion
God is the truth and reality
His truth is so strong that no one can disagree
Truth has consequences just like a tree is followed by a shadow
God's truth is that He created a world that He still sustains from time ago
 Judgement day will come tomorrow
A day for the disbelievers of hardship and sorrow
And there will be a hellfire with no water or ice
Then criminals for their evil will pay a price
So worship God and that is sound advice
And gain the knowledge of God that is precise
Then from paradise, you will get a slice
When unbelievers will enter hellfire for their vice

Mysa Elsheikh

The Spirit as a Tool to Know God

The truth of God comes from realising the existence of God, and this comes from the ability to recognise God and others outside the self by using the spirit. The spirit is a human sense just like the eyes, which allow people to see, the ears, which allow people to hear sound, and the tongue, which allows us to taste food. The spirit allows us to recognise things other than the self, and since no one is God in Islam, this shows the imperative need of the spirit to know God. Those with a sense of the spirit will recognise God, and those without a sense of the spirit may ignore His existence. This is why the problem may not be that God doesn't exist, but that people lack the tool or spirit of recognising that God exists. This is why, despite the fact that religion is truth, it is not usually considered a science, and while Islam, on the other hand, in Arab history was recognised as a science, religion is usually counted as a humanity subject with art, literature, and poetry, as they also depend on the sense of spirit, meaning, and appreciation of the other's existence.

For instance, if a goat falls into a well, the other goats do not cry after it, and they do not even make an effort to bring it out. However, if a man falls into a well, other men will gather around him; some may start crying as a form of sympathy, and others will make an effort to bring him out of the well. This caring nature of humans, of recognising others other than themselves and sharing with them their emotions, is the spirit aspect working. The spirit is a beautiful nature of humans, and its weakness or absence is a great problem, as people then would not empathise with others and would be more daring to even hurt them.

The Spirit is a gift that is passed down to a child when their parents are cousins or related. This is why people throughout history and all over the world married their relatives. The idea of paternal cousin parents is to allow an individual to understand metaphors, relative comparisons (*giyas*), and *mathal* (metaphor), that are the basis of the spirit. There cannot be a spirit in humans without parents of the same origin, there cannot be spirituality without spirit, and there cannot be religion without spirituality. This is because *giyas* (relative comparison) requires a point of comparison—a stable star to compare the moon's light to, or a point from which other points are measured. In cousin marriages, the parents are similar in blood and flesh, and this gives the person born from such a marriage a oneness with themselves that allows them to empathise with others. For example, if they see another person crying, they would behave as though they were also harmed, and so they would cry too. With marriages of different or blood strangers, the child comes from two different entities, and thus they lack a oneness that would cause them to empathise with others, and so they fail to understand others by relating with them, so they either have no spirit or a weak spirit. The fact that people no longer marry cousins in places like the west, caused an increase in people being irreligious, with some even becoming atheists who refuse to acknowledge the existence of God.

The act of the spirit, *ruh*, is to be able to cause the mind to think about something other than the self. This is why they called it *ruh*, which literally means 'the going'. This is like what goes forth or squirts to travel further or project away from source. This requires the person to be one with himself/herself, as the act of the spirit requires the person to be unified, and with both parents being similar, this is possible. But when each parent is different, the person isn't one with himself/herself but rather dual and cannot be a point of comparison to other things. This was the challenge Prophet Ismael faced. Other prophets faced and overcame similar struggles, like Jonah in the inside of the fish, Joseph in prison, and Ibrahim in the fire, but Ismael was in the inside of his body. He was half Persian from his Persian father, Abraham, and half African from his African mother, Hagar. However, it wasn't doom, as God accepted him at the end. When Abraham was told that God believed Ismael was not a human with a spirit and must be given euthanasia and killed, Ismael accepted the truth and reality of his situation and laid down for his father to be slaughtered. When God accepted that Ismael understood His point of view, Ismael proved that he received the spirit of understanding something other than himself. So God quickly abrogated the law against Ismael, and he was pardoned. Instead, an animal was slaughtered as a form of *dahiya* (sacrifice). The slaughter in Eid-adha is an act of the spirit as with people of religion, it's the flag showing spirituality. Therefore, to be mugged and refuse to give a wristwatch instead of getting stabbed and risking death is not only unacceptable, but it's an act of lacking the spirit. To accept other things to be given in place of harm to the self shows spirit and dignity. The sheep represented the body of Ismael and was slaughtered in his stead. God says, 'Whoever is not interested in the pure religion of Abraham has affirmed to themselves triviality' (2:130). Hence, those who consider themselves to be below or not worthy of *fida* or do *daha* (sacrifice) on its behalf lack spirituality, as they consider themselves to be in lower statues compared to their expensive possessions. The reason not all children of cousin parents are religious is because, to believe in the existence of God is one thing, and to be devoted to Him is another.

The children of cousin marriages not only know God because they have the spirit, but they also know God through the understanding of purity. The child of relatives comes from parents similar in blood and flesh, and the joining of similarities makes it pure, so when the creation is pure, then the creator is also pure, and so they recognise a pure God. However, when parents are strangers and are not blood related, it's the coming together of what is different, and that's an impurity, so it suggests that the creator is impure or the pure creator doesn't exist. So, the Quran (in chapter thirty-three verse fifty) makes cousin marriage obligatory, and two verses later, forbids marrying strange women.

The spirit is the blind man's cane, which connects him to other objects and helps him decide how to deal with them, how to walk around them, or how to have them moved. The spirit is what connects us to other things other than ourselves, such as recognising people beside ourselves and knowing God as outside of our humanity. It is important to connect with others, and call them in times of emergency and urgency, expecting our words to reach them. A beggar expects their words to reach the ears and hearts of people and hopes they influence them to give, and a mother hopes her kind words reach her child. Likewise, God sent a book, expecting it to be accepted by humanity. This distance between beings is a link that is established with the spirit.

In summary, believers in God are not deluded; rather, they are born believers, which is known as '*fitrah*'—the reflexive or innate belief that Muhammed (pbuh) said was the original religion for all humans before being indoctrinated and biased towards religion by parents. Like a child of cousin marriage, God's existence is forced, but acceptance of Him isn't. Belief in God comes with who we are, and it certainly doesn't mean the religion we were born into. The author of The God Delusion argues that children should not be considered to be part of and enjoy the practice of the teachings of their parent's religion. This is a form of spiritual neglect, and it breeds child negligence if parents are not allowed to take their children to church or the mosque but leave them alone at home or in other rooms while they worship. He is a man who is not only arguing outside of his expertise, but he is also dangerous to old family values.

The God Discovery argues that the idea of God isn't a delusion, like a poor mother boiling rocks in a pot for her hungry children, expecting them to believe it's real food, and waiting for it to cook until they go to sleep. This is the definition of a delusion: a lie used to allude to a more palatable reality. Those who believe God is a delusion, that believers find the world of disease, injury, death, and loss to be overwhelming, start to make up their own entities giving them superhuman strengths and abilities, and this main entity they then call God, and they then show love and devotion towards him as a form of thankfulness and gratitude for giving them so much comfort in this world. Believing he will be there to show miracles in times of need and hope; that he will be present if there's an afterlife to save them from any dangers there, including terrible eternal hellfire. However, humans do know that comforting stories, fairytales, myths, and supernatural stories exist in all human cultures, some dating back to centuries. However, humanity collectively has never considered God to be a part of the fairytales and myths of comforting the ill and cheering depressed souls. In fact, religion and fairytales have existed side by side, showing that they knew what delusions were. Those of the early generations who came across the idea of God before us, examined the evidence of Jesus, heard the words of Muhammed (pbuh), and saw Moses cross the sea, did not claim the concept of religion, which they left for their children and grandchildren, to be in reality a delusion. To call religion a delusion isn't new to our era; it was something ridiculous that was said to Muhammed to his face, as the Quran says, 'They said it was fairy-tails and legends of old.' This means that the religious teachings and documentation of the early prophets were mere old myths and legends, and works of fairytales. However, they were being ridiculous, and mocking, but they didn't believe God did not exist, as they were from cousin marriage, and they only did not accept Prophet Muhammed (pbuh) and the religion of Islam.

The spirit is also important in knowing the nature of God, if the description of God is meant to be literal or metaphorical. This is especially relevant to know since *Wahhabism* (Salafism), a sect of Islam, understands and takes verses of the Quran to be literal when traditionally they were considered metaphorical, such as God having a hand. The spirit is gentle and light, and so it understands metaphors, which are usually the condensation of information. For example, a person may wish to say that they arrived fast, but he says, he came flying instead of saying he came really, really, really fast, using really many times. This gentle understanding of metaphors is possible in having the full manifestation of the spirit. The popularity of *Wahhabism* (an extreme sect to which most terrorists belong) comes from modern society, where fewer people are marrying cousins. These stranger-to-stranger marriages produce children without the spirit who do not understand metaphors, and so they find an inclination to literal *Wahhabism*. While children from cousin marriages have natural understanding of spirit, they are inclined to the spiritual teachings of Sufism.

GOD THE PLANNER OF CREATION

The idea of God as the planner and the creator with intention, plus the idea of planned births in humanity, are the main ways to cause people to internally realise and be informed of the truth.

In Islam, we believe in absolutes. We believe that some things are absolute, not because of an original thought but because they exist as absolutes. For example, using water and salt to make salt water instead of sugar and water is absolute. That's just the way it is; it is what makes sense, and it is what anyone, anywhere, at any time in history or the future, will expect. For instance, for trees to be green is again absolute and not creative; it is not red, and it is not black, but green. The sky is blue, which is the colour of comfort. Since the sky is very high, it is further up and then further again, this is to say that the hardship of hardship, since climbing high is tiresome and that is the idea of annihilating hardship meaning comfort. Likewise, a wound, when it heals and no longer hurts, turns blueish. This is because blue is the colour of comfort. This wisdom in what God creates is because there is a plan, and it is not random creation; there is intelligence creating the world, and that is God in His wisdom. God creates nothing but the best, and nothing He creates is random; it is has been planned, as God says in the Quran, 'Blessed is God the perfect creator' (23:14).

When considering God as a creator and planner, it means considering God as causing a planned existence to materialise. It means that God identified the best form they could be in—a form not debated, not controversial, but standard and '*kun fayakon*'. He made it to be, and it came to exist. The Quran asks, 'What have those beside God created?' This is to say that God identified the best templates and forms that creation can take. God considered a red, yellow, green, purple, and brown moon, but He created a white moon to reflect light during the dark night.

CHAPTER 3

THE DESCRIPTION OF GOD

The description of God in Islam is profound. It is also impressive and authentic since it comes from the Quran, meaning it contains what God Himself describes as true and acceptable about Him. Islam came after Christianity, and Christianity came after Judaism, and all these religions believe God is one and pure (holy). But, what is important to recognise in each of these religions is that they hold further ideas that contradict this basic idea of God, except for Islam, which strictly holds on to this by negating that God has a Son, is the Trinity, or rested after creating the world which is believed literally or metaphorically by Christians and Jews.

The most important characteristic of God in Islam is that He is perfect. The Quran says, 'To God is the most perfect example' (16:60). The idea of the perfect God in Islam means that God is perfect with no shortcomings, and that God is perfect without having any bad characteristics to contradict it. The perfect God is complete in goodness without any bad characteristics. God is good as God is complete in purity and is holy, a word that is derived from the word 'whole'. God is also divine, a word derived from the word 'dive', which means to be completely submerged in water. These words describe God as good and pure.

God's completeness in purity necessary for Him to be able to create the world. God is so complete in purity and was not created and so was not joined from smaller units that it is other than Him which is joined or union, and so He was able to create the world by creating lesser particles that touched and joined to create the world. So, the creation of the world is a sign that God is complete in purity without joining or touch or descriptions of the creation. This is since God is so pure other than Him became joined to produce creation. If God was not completely pure, then the world would not have been created. This can only be true if God is perfect, so this means that the creation that is joined and put together is a sign of a God, who is complete in purity and was not created.

This belief in the perfect and pure God in Islam is why Islam is the true religion. This is because in Judaism, the

Jews believe God rested after creating the world, so their God is not perfect and gets tired. As for Christians, they believe God has a Son. This is to say God was replaced after death, and so likewise, since their God dies and has a Son, then their God is not perfect. Also, having a son associates God with sex and having children, but God is too pure to be associated with such impurities and dirt. The good God of Islam was not tired after creation, and He has no son; therefore, He is perfect and is the real God of this world. This means Islam is the true religion, and everyone must convert to Islam.

The following is a list of the most important descriptions of God in the Quran:

1. **God is Allah** - 'He is Allah the Lord' (18:38), (28:70), (59:22), (59:23), (6:3), (39:4), (23:59) and (59:24).
2. **God is One** - 'It is He a one God' (6:19), (16:51) and (14:52).
3. **God is Unique** - 'He is Unique' (112:1).
4. **God is True** - 'God is the truth' (22:6), (22:62) and (31:30).
5. **God is Alive** - 'He is alive' (40:65).
6. **God is Compassionate** - 'He is compassionate to believe in' (67:29).
7. **God knows everything** - 'He is knowledgeable of all things' (2:29), (6:101) and (57:2).
8. **God is the guardian of all directions** - 'To ever direction He is its guardian' (2:148).

9. **God is the Reliance of all** - 'He is to everything a reliance' (6:102) and (39:62)
10. **God is Guardian** - 'He is guardian' (9:51), (22:78), (2:148), (42:9) and (66:4).
11. **God is Lord of the Grand Throne** - 'He is lord of the grand throne' (9:129).
12. **God is above His creation** - 'He is above his creation' (6:18), (6:61), (30:27) and (41:15).
13. **God is Rich** - 'He is rich and has what's in the heavens and in earth' (10:68).
14. **God is quickest to account** - 'He is quickest in account' (6:62) and (13:41).
15. **God is the Lord of people** - 'He is Lord and to Him is the return' (11:34), (2:139) and (43:64).
16. **God has the right to be worshipped** - 'He has right to be worshipped and asked forgiveness' (74:56).
17. **God has signs of His divinity in the world** - 'He shows His signs' (40:13) and (40:13).
18. **God gives life and death** - 'He gives life and death' (40:68), (7:158), (10:56), (23:80), (53:44) and (44:?).
19. **God is capable of all things** - 'He is capable of all things' (42:9), (5:120), (6:17), (11:4), (30:50), (42:9), (57:2), (64:1) and (67:1).
20. **God is the Lord of Sirius** - 'He is Lord of Sirius (the Mighty Star)' (53:49).
21. **God is the creator of the heavens and earth** - 'He created the heavens and earths in six days' (57:4), (6:73) and (11:7).

22. **God is with people in all places** - 'He is with people wherever they may be' (57:4), (34:47) and (58:7).
23. **God is doing something new everyday** - 'He is everyday doing something' (55:29)
24. **God knows all sight and no sight sees Him all** - 'He knows all sight' (6:103).
25. **God is god to all** - 'He is God of all things' (6:164) and (43:84).
26. **God controls His creation** - 'There is no animal except He is in control of it' (11:56).
27. **God is unchangeable and cannot be negated** - 'He is strong in being' (13:13) and (23:88).
28. **God has beautiful Names:**
1. He Accepts all who Repent and is Merciful - 'He accepts repenting and is merciful' (2:37), (2:54), (9:104) and (9:118).
2. God is Compassionate and Merciful - 'He is compassionate and merciful' (2:163) and (59:22).
3. God is High and Mighty - 'He is high and mighty' (2:255).
4. God is Hearing and Knowledgeable - 'He is hearing and knowledgeable' (2:137), (5:76), (6:3), (6:115), (8:61), (10:65), (12:34), (21:4), (26:220), (29:5), (29:60), (41:36) and (44:6).
5. God is Forgiving and Merciful - 'He is forgiving and merciful' (10:107), (12:98), (28:16), (46:8), (42:5) and (39:53).

6. God is Strong and Dignified - 'He is strong and dignified' (11:66) and (42:19).
7. God is Knowledgeable and Wise - 'He is knowledgeable and wise' (12:83), (12:100), (51:30) and (66:2).
8. God is the Creator and Knowledgeable - 'He is the creator and knowledgeable' (15:86) and (36:?).
9. God is Hearing and Seeing - 'He is Hearing and Seeing' (17:1), (40:20), (40:56) and (42:11).
10. God is High and Great - 'He is Hight and Great' (22:62) and (42:4).
11. God is the Truth and Clear - 'He is the Clear Truth' (24:25).
12. God is Dignified and Wise 'He is dignified and wise' (14:4), (29:26), (29:42), (31:9), (34:27), (59:24), (16:60), (53:2), (45:37), (57:1), (61:1) and (62:3).
13. God is Rich and Grateful - 'He is rich and grateful' (31:26), (35:15), (57:24) and (60:6).
14. God is High and Great - 'He is high and great' (31:30) and (34:23).
15. God is One and Oppresses - 'He is one and oppress' (4:39) and (13:16).
16. God is Dignified and Forgiving - 'He is dignified and forgiving' (39:5) and (67:2).
17. God is Faithful - 'He is faithful' (42:9).
18. God is the Dignified and Merciful - 'He is dignified and merciful' (44:42), (26:9), (26:68), (26:104),

(26:122), (26:140), (26:159), (26:175), (26:191), (30:5) and (44:?).

19. God is the Wise and Knowledgeable - 'He is wise and knowledgeable' (51:30); 'God is Wise and Informed' (6:18), (34:1), (6:73) and (43:84).
20. God is the Sustainer and Strong and firm - 'He is the sustainer and is strong and firm' (51:58).
21. God is Obeyed and Merciful - 'He is obeyed and merciful' (52:28).
22. God is the First and Last and the Apparent and Hidden (57:3).
23. God is the Creator and gives Forms - 'He is the creator and giver of form' (59:24).
24. God is Gentle and Informed - 'He is gentle and informed' (6:103) and (67:14).
25. God is Merciful - 'He is the most Merciful' (12:64) and (12:92).
26. God is Dignified and Knowledgeable - 'He is dignified and knowledgeable' (27:78).
27. God is Knowledgeable and Capable - 'He is knowledgeable and wise' (30:54).
28. God is Merciful and Forgiving - 'He is merciful and forgiving' (34:2).
29. God is the Opener and Knowledgeable - 'He is the opener and knowledgeable' (34:26).
30. God is Forgiving and Loving - 'He is forgiving and loving' (85:14).

CHAPTER 4

THE NECESSITY OF GOD

The necessity of God means there is a need for God to exist based on the evidence, but as humans, we also need God to exist. This need is necessary because of the benefits we gain from God, such as help in times of need. God says in the Quran, 'The one who answers the prayer of emergencies to remove harm' (27:62).

The necessity of the existence of God affects human behaviour and morality. When people say God is pure, they imply they won't rape people. When they say God is one, they mean they believe hardship is to be relieved and that they also will help people in need. And when they say the good God exists, that is to say they will do good to others. This is because God is pure, as He was not created by sex, and so it will inspire them to be chaste and avoid raping people. The one true God is powerful to help us in times of hardship; however, many other gods share the power of God and thus each god becomes very weak and cannot help us overcome our hardship. This means believing in one God makes the person insistent on helping others in times of need. The idea that God is good makes Him a role model for doing good to everyone. Doing good deeds without believing in God negates the greater good of God, so it means they don't believe in the greater good, even if they claim to do some acts of good.

God inspires people to be good, and while it is possible for unbelievers in God to be moral and do good, religion and heaven give people an extra incentive to do good. God says that those who deny religion are those who mistreat orphans and are not keen on feeding the poor (107:1-3). This association between morality and religion is so strong that in Sudan, they have a saying that says, 'Be afraid of the one who is not afraid of God.'

CHAPTER 5

THE EVIDENCE OF GOD (SIGNS OF GOD)

The signs of God are signposts or marks that describe God and suggest that they were created by God. Therefore, knowing the signs, we come to believe that God exists. The Quran, the Holy Book of Islam, which is the speech of God, is a miracle that came to Prophet Muhammed (pbuh) via the angel Gabriel. The Quran lists many signs of God throughout the holy book to affirm the existence of God. Then again, who better to say God exists than God Himself? The many strong signs of the Islamic God in the world mean that Islam is seen as a true religion, and its knowledge is recognised as a science other than superstitious omens—especially since the signs of God fit the description of God in Islam, meaning the Islamic God is the true Lord of the worlds.

The great proof of the existence of God and religion means that the belief or disbelief in Islam must be taken seriously since it affects this life and the afterlife. In Islamic law, disbelief is punishable by death, and God rewards the believers with an eternal life of bliss. The Quran itself is a sign of God, since it is God's speech organised with numbers. In the Quran, each chapter and verse has a number, and how God names the chapter or what God says in a verse all correspond to the meaning of this number. The Quran is an accurate speech that respects numbers —the strongest idea in existence. This is proof that it came from a great and powerful authority, that can only be God. This means, by definition, the Quran is the speech of God, just as the sky is blue. The nonbelievers in Prophet Muhammed (pbuh) time said that the Quran is the beautiful and that God exist; however, Muhammed (pbuh) fraud it, saying that God did not send him (Muhammed (pbuh)) or authorise it, but Muhammed (pbuh) said it in God's name without God's permission.

The world is a place of testing people on religion, so that it has wild animals, volcanoes, and disease, the things of the hellfire to warn from it, and it has honey, gold and musk; the things of heaven to attract to it. The world has things from hell and things from heaven to be an exhibit of the afterlife. God created the things in the world to

The Discovery of God

give us an idea about who He is, and these things give ideas related to God that they are signs of God. God also names each chapter of the Quran after one of these things or objects, for example the cave, which is a hole in the mountain. Mountains are joining of lesser stones, and so they are union and impure, but a hole in them means purity, so caves are a sign of God.

The clarity of God's signs creates belief, and so there is a legitimate punishment in Sharia Law for disbelief and atheism, as well as those who do not believe in the existence of God and refuse His religion of Islam. Ignorance is thus a killer. This makes the knowledge of the signs of God worthy of saving the people in this world and from eternal hellfire punishment. The spread of the signs of God encompasses a grand God. God says in the Quran, 'He will show His signs in the horizon and in their selves' (41:53).

Signs are also important in the medical field, as they aid in the diagnosis of diseases. Signs are important in solving crimes, where footprints and thumbprints are taken as proof for wrongdoings and conviction and punishing people. Likewise, signs have weight and value in religion to affirm the existence of God and merit His worship in this world. Also, signs of God have traditionally been considered to contain the power of healing in prophetic medicine. God says in the Quran, 'Praise to God, God will show His signs until people understand and believe' (27:93). The Quran is also called, *ayat Allah*, meaning 'signs of God' in Arabic, as it contains the proof of God.

To understand the Quran, a person must first understand numbers, for numbers have meanings; the numbers used for the chapters and individual verses in the Quran have additional meaning and power. For instance, the number one means being first, at the top, or important, and the number two means couple, a relationship, or joining, and the number three symbolises harm since three lines join to make a triangle that has pointed and sharp corners that can harm. In this chapter, we will go through the Quran chapter by chapter and list its numbers and what they mean, as well as how they are a sign and proof of God. Understanding the congruity of numbers in the Quran is a miracle and is proof it came from an all-knowledgeable God, Allah.

> Consider how boats from the thirsty tree find much water in the sea
> Or how sweet honey comes from the small bee
> Or that prophets give us knowledge without taking a fee
> Or how God provides sustenance from foods like potatoes, carrots and pea
> Or how God gives us senses to be safe such as hearing and to see
> Is such a God not worthy to be prayed to, as we fall to our knee
> And to testify He is one, and not two or three

Signs of God mentioned in the Quran
The open

The first chapter of the Quran is called 'the open'. This means what is open, and not closed and difficult. So 'the opened' means what is easy and accessible. The number one means important or critical, and God says the most part of life is easy and that things are open, so He named the first chapter 'the open'. This is the case since a good God exists. The easy state of life, and the lack of problems in most instances are all proof of the existence of God.

THE COW

The second chapter of the Quran is called 'the cow'. The number two means to meet, touch, or join, which means stimuli. The cow is an animal that is known to only eat, drink, and mate and then sit there for long periods of time doing nothing. The Quran also counts the cow as a sign of God, which means there are many things to sense and become aware of in the world. This makes the cow a sign of God. The Prophet Muhammed (pbuh) said, 'The meat of the cow is illness and its milk is healing.' This is to affirm the need for firm stimuli, as it is symbolised by cow meat, which is a sign of dumb awareness of disease. It is possible that too much beef is a risk factor for illness. However, milk, on the other hand, symbolises knowledge, meaning accurate awareness; therefore, milk is health. The cows also represent rest and ease, as they like to sit and rest, and the state of no harm is a sign of God.

THE FAMILY OF JOACHIM

This is the third chapter of the Quran. Joachim is the family of Jesus, whose mother was Mary. The number three means harm since three lines that join create a triangle that has sharp and pointed corners. The idea of harm to God is the great impurity of an intimate relationship of sex; therefore, it means God chose Joachim, who are pure in relations, to be the family of Jesus. The family of Joachim has Jesus, John the Baptist, and the Virgin Mary, to mention a few who are all famous for their ideas of purity.

The family of Joachim is a sign of God, since pure relations are signs of God. When a person is born from a pure relation, they are created in purity, and purity is a sign of a pure creator—God. Therefore, God counts the family of Joachim as a sign of God in the Quran. Joachim in Arabic is Imran, from *am raan* (literally view of uncle" meaning, performs cousin marriage, which is commanded by the Quran (33:50). Cousin marriages are pure relations since they are similar, so it's a joining of similarities, while stranger's marriage is the joining of different people making the marriage impure. Impure relations suggest an impure creator, which means no pure God exists, so they are forbidden in Islam (Quran 33:52).

THE WOMEN

The fourth chapter of the Quran is called 'women'—the female human. The number four means awareness and knowledge since four lines make the four corners of a square when joined. This corner can be felt, so it means knowledge. This is the opposite of a circle, which is smooth and doesn't have corners to feel. God chose women to be the fourth chapter name since women are designed with great wisdom and filled with the truth of God. The female body shows knowledge of purity, which is the proof of God.

Women are a sign of God, since their bodies have a plan of purity, meaning their physical form is filled with pure ideas that support belief in a pure God, Allah, the God of Islam. This pure plan is a lack of joining of different or meeting of opposites. This is in the human face, which has a nose that looks like a male genitalia and a mouth that looks like the female genitalia, the nose is a long and protruding flesh, that looks like a penis connected to the eyes that are like testicles. The human mouth is an opening that is internal to the level of the human face like a vagina. The male nose and female mouth are different and opposite, so they are separated where the moustache grows in males. This is a plan of purity, as it separates different and opposite to remain pure. As women in the middle of their bodies, in their genitalia, have absence of flesh (no penis) and men have presence of flesh (a penis), it means women genitalia shadow or repeat the absence of the face (where the male looking nose is separated from female looking mouth) and this gives further proof for a pure creator God. This means women are a sign of God in Islam. The Prophet Muhammed (pbuh) said he marries women, and whoever doesn't marry a woman is not of his people. Prophet Muhammed (pbuh) said of this world he loves women and that men should be kind to women. This association of women with religion was transgressed when pagans started to worship female gods, and the Quran says some disbelievers believed angels were female. Catholics are said to worship Mary, the mother of Jesus, or hold her in high regards, a notion that is sometimes referred to as the divine feminine.

THE FEAST

The feast is the fifth chapter of the Quran. The number five means support since the hand has five fingers, together with the four limbs and the head, which make five protrusions on the body. God chose the feast, which means much eating, to be the fifth chapter since eating food is a sign of God. This is because the face has a nose, which looks like a male genitalia, and a mouth, which looks like a female genitalia, and these two are forever separated in the place where the moustache is supposed to grow to mean purity; this is the character of God. God the pure emphasises and confirms to people the separation between the male looking nose and female looking mouth, of the face by eating, which cuts and separates the food into parts. Since God does not allow a human to live unless they confirm purity by the cutting of the food to support the truth of separating the male from the female in the face. Therefore, God counted eating to cut food much such as in a feast as a sign of God. The Quran counts the story of when Angels visited prophet Abraham (as) and the angels did not eat from the food he offered and he was shocked and scared by this reaction as it is not human and unnatural. This chapter of the Quran, also mentions Jesus and his disciples feast from heaven.

THE CATTLE

Cattle is the sixth chapter of the Quran. The number six is the number three twice, and three, as we mentioned earlier, means harm, and thus six means much harm. Cattle are harmful animals, as they can attack with their horns or kick. However, since they are eaten as food and eating is a sign of God, the much cattle in the world is a sign of God.

THE PLATFORM

The number seven is five plus two. Also, two fives equal ten, meaning complete giving; thus, five and two is knowledge of ten or a symbol. Therefore, seven is a beautiful number, and so the heavens are seven in Islam. The seventh chapter of the Quran is the platform since it is an elevation and anything placed upon it is easily seen to give knowledge of it. Since God is a pure creator, it is obvious that the reality of the idea of making things obvious and elevated in platform is also a sign of the high God. In this chapter, God mentions a platform between heaven and hell where some people will stand and be judged before being admitted to heaven. Raising people in awards and social status is indeed a sign of much goodness and is a sign of the good God.

THE BOOTY

The booty is the eighth chapter of the Quran. You get the number eight when you add five plus three. Five depicts the hand, which means giving, and three is harm, so giving in harm means taking the booty in war, which are the leftovers of war from the lost army. This giving in times of death and loss, shows that good things still exist in hardship, and this is a sign of the existence of God.

THE REPENTANCE

The ninth chapter of the Quran is repentance. Since five means giving, ten implies perfect giving (two times five). Nine is one less than ten, so it means a wrong, an error, or something that is not right or perfect. So the ninth chapter is what a person does when they do wrong and must repent. In Islam, God is considered perfect; therefore, Muslims fast in the ninth month of the lunar calendar called Ramadan. This is because the moon represents the idea of giving as it gives light in the dark night, and since God gives, the ninth month suggests an error in giving or an imperfect God, so Muslims fast as a way to appreciate and affirm the perfection of God. Muslims then celebrate the beginning of the tenth month, called Eid. Since ten means perfect giving, the tenth moon means the perfect giver. The Prophet Muhammed (pbuh) taught Muslims to say a prayer during the nights of the month of Ramadan. This prayer is: 'Lord of forgiveness and pardon and generosity who loves to pardon, so pardon us.'

The act of repentance, where people ask for pardon and forgiveness after an error, is a sign of God. The desire to repent shows the importance of being good, which is the character of God. In many countries, nine is part of the emergency number since it connotes a serious problem.

JONAH

The tenth chapter of the Quran is named Jonah after Prophet Jonah who was swallowed by a fish. The number ten is perfect giving, since it is two fives and five is the number of giving, and therefore the hand that takes and gives has five fingers. The perfect giving, is to give when life is in danger and death is imminent. This is the story of Jonah, who did not die in the fish but lived. The tenth chapter is about Prophet Jonah, who gained life after risking it and that shows the overwhelming goodness of God.

HUD

The eleventh chapter of the Quran is Hud, named after Prophet Hud. Hud was an Arab prophet, and his name means 'guider', 'giver of guidance', or 'guided'. Eleven is one plus ten, and it means giving what is important or giving advice and guidance on what is right. The eleventh chapter means advice giving or guidance, which is the work of prophets who advise people to worship God to avoid hellfire. An example of such prophets is prophet Hud, after whom the chapter was named.

God giving guidance and knowledge of the truth and what is right is a sign of His existence. This is because God is good, and advice guides us to what is good.

Prophet Hud was sent to the people of Add, who were Arabs and lived in southern Arabia. When they refused to obey Prophet Hud and instead believe and worship God, God sent strong winds to their valleys that destroyed them and left them dead and extinct.

JOSEPH

The twelfth chapter of the Quran is Joseph. Ten means perfect giving, since five means giving and ten is double five. The number two means pair, relationship, or mating, and therefore the overall meaning of twelve is choosing perfect relationships. The twelfth chapter is named after Joseph, who refused the sexual advances of his master's wife and preferred to keep sex inside marriage. This act of purity is a sign of the existence of the pure God. In

Islam, sex has to be inside marriage only, and therefore all nakedness and shows of affection in public are not allowed. Thus, women cover their bodies in what is called the *hijab*. This purity is a sign of the pure good God, Allah.

THE THUNDER

The thirteenth chapter of the Quran is called thunder. Thirteen is the addition of ten (perfect giving) and three (harm) which overall implies harm in perfect giving. This loud sound that can harm during rain attracts attention to the giving of rain, which is the mercy as it waters plants and creates lakes and rivers for animals and people to drink. The thunder is thus a celebration of life and the blessing of rain; thus, this is a sign of God, who is good, and therefore creates a celebration of what gives life.

ABRAHAM

The fourteenth chapter of the Quran is Abraham. Abraham is considered the father of the prophets since Jewish prophets such as Jesus and Moses, as well as Prophet Muhammed (pbuh) are all from his progeny. Abraham was the first prophet to preach that God was pure, and he believed that the pure God created a pure plan for the world and purity in the human form. This meant Abraham rejected worshipping impure gods that showed shortcomings, such as the sun and moon, which disappear at the end of the day or month. He also rejected worshipping statues because they were created by men and, hence, impure. These statues also lack the ability to hear, see, have insight, or protect themselves from danger. Therefore, Abraham broke all these worshipped statues and left a remainder of the statues to mock their false religion.

Abraham is chapter fourteen in the Quran, and fourteen is the addition ten and four. Ten symbolises perfect giving, and four symbolises awareness or touch, so together, fourteen means the giving of awareness or wisdom. Since Abraham knew well of the purity of God, it is the perfect awareness or wisdom. For instance, Abraham understood and identified the correct touch and pure nature of God and built the house of God in Mecca. Abraham said God is just like the middle part of our bodies, which is covered and hasn't been touched, so he travelled to the mid-west of Arabia, which means dark and covered. This is how Abraham discovered the house of God, a valley set around many mountains. Mountains symbolise the joining and touching of two or more hills, so they are impure; however, the valley is the absence of that, so it is pure. So Abraham built a house of God in the mid-west of Arabia, in Mecca. Abraham also married his cousin Sarah, who is a pure relative, and almost slaughtered his son Ishmael as he was not born from a cousin marriage, so he was impure and had difficulty realising the pure God.

THE STONE

The fifteenth chapter of the Quran is the stone. The number fifteen is equal to ten plus five. Ten means perfect giving, and five means support or lesser giving, so the complete meaning of fifteen is support for perfect giving. The stone is made up of smaller parts joined together, making it impure, so smaller stones are a sign of purity in the world. So the existence of small clumps of earth, which are small stones, a sign of purity and therefore a sign of the existence of the pure God.

In Islamic law, adulterers are stoned to death to teach them not to be greedy with sex, since that small joinery is purity and good. In Hajj (the greater pilgrimage), stones are hit where the devil tried to trick Abraham into killing his son Ishmael as was commanded by God since he was impure and created from parents of different origins and not cousins who are similar and related. In the house of God, there is the Black Stone, which is used to emphasise the purity of the house of God. The Black Stone is said to have come from heaven and was initially white but turned black from the many sins of people.

THE BEE

The sixteenth chapter of the Quran is the bee. The bee is a small insect that can fly. All insects have small bodies, so they carry meanings of no touch or less joining, which is pure. This makes insects symbols of purity and a sign of the pure God. The bee emphasises its meaning by shaking like a person moving a lot so as not to be touched. It also makes a sound of disappointment when touched after moving. The bee is very organised, as it lives in man-made houses, in mountains, or in trees. The bee produces honey, which in the Quran is considered to heal to disease.

Sixteen is the addition of ten (perfect giving) and six (double harm), so six is too much harm (666 is said to be the number of the devil); bees also sting, explaining the harm it brings. The Prophet Muhammed (pbuh) said the chapter of the bee can be read for all adversities in life to improve every situation in life, such as to cure leprosy and insanity.

THE NIGHT JOURNEY

The seventeenth chapter of the Quran is the night journey. Arabs used to travel at night as it was cooler. Also, Prophet Muhammed travelled to Jerusalem during the night in the company of angel Gabriel on a donkey like celestial animal called *Burag* that flew them to Levent and then up the heavens until they reached the end of the created world and saw God. Travelling from one place to another is a sign of God, since it reveals the vastness of the created world and therefore the greatness of God.

THE CAVE

The eighteenth chapter of the Quran is the cave. Eighteen is the combination of ten (perfect giving), five (lesser giving), and three (harm), so the overall meaning is that of giving of harm in the perfect giving. This is similar to a hole in a mountain since harm usually means absent or causes absence. Mountains are a combination of lesser hills so they are impure. However, a hole in the mountain is purity, since it is the absence of impurity of the mountain; therefore, caves are a sign of God. Prophet Muhammed (pbuh) received the Quran for the first time during his stay, meditating inside a cave in Mecca.

MARY

The nineteenth chapter of the Quran is Mary. Nineteen is the addition of nine (imperfect or missing giving) and ten (perfect giving), so nineteen means virgin, since it is a state of a lack of giving in a relationship. Being a virgin is a state of purity and a sign of the existence of the pure God. Mary is the most famous virgin in the world and is the mother of Prophet Jesus (as), so God counts her as the nineteenth chapter of the Quran.

Mary was born after her mother prayed to have a pious and devoted child. She lived in solitude and in devotion in the temple, and she had miracles of grapes in times of no harvest and the birth of Jesus as a virgin. Virginity is sexual purity and, therefore, a sign of God.

THE CHASTE

The chaste is the twentieth chapter of the Quran. Chastity means being pure outside of marriage. It is the opposite of promiscuity, which encourages sexual relationships outside marriage. The number twenty is two times ten (perfect giving), and twice is from the word two, which means relationships. The overall meaning of twenty is a relationship that is perfect, meaning marriage. This is what a chaste person prefers. Prophet Muhammed (pbuh) said, 'God is pure and loves purity' just like many other metaphors for purity in the Quran. Therefore, the purity of chastity is a sign of God in the world.

THE PROPHETS

A sign of God are the prophets sent by God with the message of religion or with holy books. The prophets are men who were contacted by God using the angels to proclaim that He exists and should be worshipped and that there will be a judgement day; a reward of heaven or punishment of hellfire. Twenty means chastity, and the number one means important. So the overall meaning of twenty-one is a person to whom chastity is important, and those people are the pure prophets.

THE PILGRIMAGE

The pilgrimage entails travelling to check the existence of the house of God, and confirm the existence of God so that they can then be sincere and devoted in His worship. The number two means union or purity, and the number twenty emphasises ten, the perfect giving.

The overall meaning of twenty-two is the giving of purity and receiving information about God, such as what happens when visiting the house of God on pilgrimage.

In Islam, the pilgrimage involves visiting the house of God in Mecca, Arabia. Pilgrims travel to the mid-west of Arabia to check for the signs of God. Middle means union and west means dark and together, mid-west means to cover, which is an act of purity. Therefore, the house of God is located in a valley in the middle of mountains in the mid-west of Arabia. When pilgrims witness the house of God, surrounded by mountains, they recognise that it's a pure place, and so it confirms the existence of the pure God, Allah, the God of Islam.

THE BELIEVERS

The believers is the twenty-third chapter of the Quran. The believers are those who believe in God and His messenger to avoid hellfire and seek heaven and the presence of God. Three symbolises harm, and twenty emphasises perfect giving, since it is ten, twice. The believers is twenty-three since they believe in the perfect giving of heaven and refuse the harm of hellfire. The Quran considers the existence of good people who believe in God, as a sign of God. The fact that Islam is spread, and there are nearly two billion Muslims worldwide is a sign that there is truth to Islam and that God exists for all these people to believe in.

THE LIGHT

The light is chapter twenty-four. Twenty emphasises perfect giving, and four means awareness. Light therefore brings awareness to things as they are, and so it's the twenty-fourth chapter of the Quran. Light shines to show itself and what exists, and so it's a sign of the existence of God. This chapter has the famous Quranic verse: 'God is the light of the heavens and earth.' When Prophet Muhammed (pbuh) was asked if he saw God, he said, 'I see Him as light' and in another Hadith, he said, 'I saw light.'

THE LAW

The twenty-fifth chapter of the Quran is the law. This is because twenty means perfect giving emphasised and five is confirmation, since the law gives justice to what is confirmed of crimes. The law is a sign of God, and there are laws in the world that govern people's lives. These laws encourage us to do good and avoid evil. Therefore, the law is a sign of God since it calls us to do good, which is the character of God.

THE POETS

The twenty-sixth chapter of the Quran is the poets. This is because twenty is emphasise of the perfect giving and six is two threes so it means too much harm, the total meaning being giving a lot of harm, since poets show emotion and great empathy. Poets and poetry is a sign of God, since there to be understanding and compassion as in poetry is a sign of God. That it is not a mere materialistic world of animals, but there is sentiment, emotion, understanding and wisdom in the world. Therefore, poetry is a sign of God, and God mentions it in the Quran.

THE ANTS

The twenty-seventh chapter of the Quran is the ants. The ant is an organised creature that travels in ordered lines. It is a small black insect that causes swelling on the skin where it bites. Insects are made of small bodies, and since small joining is pure, this purity of the insects and especially the ant is a sign of God.

THE STORIES

The twenty-eighth chapter of the Quran is the stories. The stories are made up of the best parts of events, real or fictional, that are gathered and told to entertain or give wisdom. The fact that events can be related and organised, is a sign of the existence of a grand God who creates with a plan and gives meaning to life. Thus, the existence of stories is a sign of the existence of God. The number twenty-eight is from eight meaning comfort, since eight is five (meaning giving) and three (meaning harm) meaning giving harm or its opposite comfort, and twenty is ten twice to mean the giving of emphasis. This comfort is in stories that do not harm even when the stories are of danger or horror.

THE SPIDER

The twenty-ninth chapter of the Quran is the spider. God, in the Quran, counts the spider as a sign of God. All insects support the existence of the pure God, as explained in previous chapters. The number twenty-nine is a combination of nine (one less than ten -meaning imperfect) and twenty (proper giving), and this is to say what is imperfect or reduced in giving (such as being small) and this symbolises the spider, which is gentle and not heavy. The presence of the spider's web outside the cave where Prophet Muhammed (pbuh) protected him since the disbelieving enemies did not believe there will be someone inside the cave.

THE ROMANS

The Romans are one of the six human races, which include the Africans, Arabs, Persians, Indians, and Asians. In Arabic, 'Romans' is another word for the Caucasian race or the Europeans. God also counts the Romans as a sign of God since they are white and blonde people, and this white colour is a sign of purity. This is because white is the colour of light, and it is not made up of different other colours, so that makes it pure. Thus, the existence of white people is a sign of the existence of a pure creator, God. Caucasians, or Romans, are a race of humans who represent the idea of creation in humans, therefore they are rich and with developed countries, so for them to be white further proves a pure creator.

LUQMAN

Luqman, a wise prophet, is counted a sign of God in the Quran. This is because wisdom is also a sign of God. Wisdom informs us of what is important, and the appreciation and value of wisdom is a sign that God, rich in wisdom, exists. Luqman is chapter thirty-one of the Quran. Thirty-one is the combination of thirty (perfect giving and thrice harm) and one (first or important), so together it means avoiding what gives harm. Wisdom improves life, and makes things better by advising what is best. The chapter of Luqman containing signs of God, such as the advice Luqman gives to his son.

THE PROSTRATION

The prostration means lowering the human face to the ground. This placing of the face to the ground is part of the prayer in Islam, and it is in the direction of the House of God in Mecca. The human face was purely planned, since the nose looks like a male and the mouth looks like a female, and they are separated in the space where the moustache grows in males. This is a sign that the human is created by God and that God is pure and holy. Placing the face on the ground in prostration is an act of acceptance of the face since the ground means acceptance; it prints back a response, and this is like following command and being acceptable.

Prostration was a curtsy to great kings just like the Quran counts the prostration of Joseph's family to

Joseph in Egypt to make his dream come true. In Islam, prostration is exclusively done to God alone since He created the face and is therefore most deserving of it. The prostration is chapter thirty-two in the Quran. Thirty is ten (perfect giving), and it is three times and three means harm, and two means union. The total meaning is thirty means three tens meaning what give harm or hardship such as bending and lowering down, and two means what has union which is the face that has union of the female mouth and male nose. Together it means the lowering down of the face, which is prostration.

THE GROUPS

The groups is chapter thirty-three. Thirty means to give pain, since ten is great giving and three is harm and adding to that another three also means pain, so the meaning of thirty-three is major pain. Groups of people are capable of causing great problems or harm. A group is made up of many people usually of similar opinions. In the Quran says God, 'The group of God is the victorious.' The parties, sects, and groups of people gathering is a sign of God. This is because people are good, and many people working together brings a greater good, which is a sign of God.

SHEBA

The tribe of Sheba in Arabia is also counted as a sign of God. Arabs are a race that represents the mind among human races. This means that they are mindful people who avoid harm to survive in the desert. The tribe of Sheba is called *Saba* in Arabic, which is translated as 'refuse harm'. This is to say that they strongly refuse harm, and therefore they are good people, which makes them a sign of the good God.

God is good and perfect. He refuses harm, wrong, and error, and so the Arab tribe carrying this character is a sign of God. The chapter of Sheba is number thirty-four; thirty is three multiplied by ten, which means causing harm. And four is awareness; thus, the total meaning of thirty-four is to be aware of any harm caused. This meaning corresponds to the character of the tribe of Sheba.

THE EXISTENCE

All that exists is a sign of God, since God is the creator behind it. This is the commonest argument to the existence of God. The thirty-fifth chapter of the Quran is existence. Thirty is three multiplied by ten, which means causing harm. Five also means giving, so this is to say that what can be harmed (meaning creation) or what there is a lot of to be a burden to create by humans and therefore must be created by a powerful God.

THE IMPOSSIBLE

The impossible is the thirty-sixth chapter of the Quran. In Arabic, it is called *Yaasin*. Thirty-six equals three (harm) multiplied by ten (giving) plus six (also harm), so overall it means impossible, since what is impossible is of great harm or difficult to achieve.

Life is not a random creation, as evolutionists claim it to be; instead, it has been organised by God. They believe that with randomness, anything is possible and can be created, but any difficulty or impossibility met means that only God can select what will happen. That absoluteness in saying that some things are difficult or impossible to create is a sign of organisation, control, and selection of God. Therefore, some things being difficult or impossible is a sign of God.

THE ROWS

The rows is the thirty-seventh chapter of the Quran. Rows are lines, which come one after another. The soldiers or any organisation of rows is a sign of God. One straight line is good, and another after that is a greater good and a sign of the good God. Ten (perfect giving) multiplied by three (harm) means something that is overwhelming, and seven is wisdom. This means the overwhelming wisdom is to be straight, accept good things and reject harm, which is what rows symbolise. This makes rows a sign of God.

THE SPECIFIC

The specific is the thirty-eighth chapter of the Quran. The specific is opposite in meaning to the word random or vague, and things being specific is all a sign of the existence of God. This is because specificity is a sign of purity, while admixtures represent impurity. Therefore, for things to be specific is a sign of God. The specific is chapter thirty-eight because thirty equals ten (giving) times three (harm), which together means overwhelming or burden. Eight also equals three (harm) times five (giving), and together they refer to harm giving or clueing to comfort. This is because when something is specific, it is overwhelming in its identity, which makes it safe. This is because when it is known for what it is, it can be dealt with, but something with a mixed or unspecific identity can be difficult to recognise and can be harmful. This is like not knowing if a rope is a snake or rope, when it's identify is specified it is safer to deal with, preserving life.

THE TROOPS

The armies or troops is the name of chapter thirty-nine of the Quran. They fight for life, and the need to preserve what is good such as life, is a sign of the good God. Thirty-nine equals ten (perfect giving) times three (harm), which overall means it's overwhelming in harm. Nine is a shortcoming of ten, from perfect giving meaning a shortcoming in death after life. The overall meaning of thirty-nine is overwhelming harm, which means the soldiers kill and cause death.

THE FORGIVEN

'Forgiven' is a sign of God when an injustice has happened and it is forgiven. The sign that people don't want further harm to happen as the punishment of criminals and hate doing wrong even to their worst enemy is a sign of God. The fact that people hate harm and want good things is a sign of the good God. The number forty is made of four tens; ten is perfect giving, and four is awareness. So forty means those who are aware of the importance of giving, hate harm, and forgive when wronged.

THE VERDICT

The verdict, which is a judgement or opinion, is the most important fact. God is important so verdict is a sign of important knowledge. The verdict is to consider the most beneficial thing, what has the most goodness for people. And being keen on good is a sign of the existence of the good God. Forty-one is the number of this chapter, the verdict in the Quran. Forty is four times ten plus one; four is awareness, ten is perfect giving, and one is important. The overall meaning of forty-one is giving important knowledge, which is the verdict. The Quran, in many instances, is full of verdicts on the issues of life, be it breastfeeding, divorce, or inheritance, and God's verdict is acceptable to the believers.

THE ADVICE

The advice is to tell someone what is best, most beneficial, or important about an issue. This giving of advice is to give what is best, and this is a sign of the appreciation of something good, which is the character of God; hence, advice is a sign of God. The advice is the forty-second chapter of the Quran because forty is four times ten plus two; four means being aware, ten is perfect giving, and two is union or what produces, so the overall meaning is the awareness of giving something fruitful, which is what advice is.

THE ORNAMENT

The ornament is the beauty that is on many objects, buildings, and even the body, such as henna. The ornament is chapter forty-three, which is equal to four times ten plus three. Ten means perfect giving, four is awareness, and three is harm or difficulty. So the overall meaning is to be aware of giving something that is difficult. This is because the swirls, flowers, and geometric shapes can be difficult to give meaning to or make sense of. The ornament is a sign of God since it's a sign of a greater meaning and beauty in existence, and that is the existence of God.

THE SMOKE

The smoke is a sign of God in the Quran. This is because in the midst of the destruction by fire, which happens by joining and friction between different an impurity, a white smoke is raised to symbolise goodness, since white is the colour of purity and goodness. This makes smoke a message of goodness that is created by the destructive fire, that destroys the impure friction of wood. This emphasis on good things and wisdom is a sign of the existence of God, according to the Quran. The smoke is chapter forty-four, which is equal to four (awareness or wisdom) times ten (the awareness of giving). So together, forty-four is providing wisdom, which is what smoke from the fire represents.

THE KNEELING

The Quran counts people kneeling as a sign of God. This is because kneeling is a sign of being overwhelmed, in shock, or overcomed while saying that greater things exist. The kneeling is chapter forty-five, meaning four (awareness) multiplied by ten (perfect giving) plus five (giving or confirmed). This is overall giving that it's a lot, meaning overwhelming to cause kneeling. In western cultures, men kneel when proposing marriage to a woman to say that without a wife, they will be overwhelmed by hardship. According to the Quran, Judgement Day will be so overwhelming that people will fall to their knees.

THE VALLEY

The valley is a sign of God because mountains are made of the joining of smaller entities, making them impure, but the empty space between them makes the valley pure, and so it's a sign of a pure God. The house of God is in the valley of Mecca, but the chapter's name in Arabic is *Ahgaf*, meaning a valley in southern Arabia. This lower valley carries signs of God since the south emphasises union, and so it has stronger signs of purity than other valleys in the world.

The valley is chapter forty-six; forty equals four (awareness) multiplied by ten (perfect giving), plus six (three twice), which means too much harm. So the overall meaning of forty-six is what gives great awareness meaning mountain, since it is a lot to be aware of, and six is too much harm so meaning missing since harm is usually missing or would want to be missing, so the overall meaning describes a valley.

MUHAMMED

Muhammed (pbuh) is a sign of God in the Quran. Prophet Muhammed (pbuh) was born into pure marriages. He was born from a cousin marriage; his mother's third grandfather and his father's fifth grandfather were Kilab bin Murrah. The man was born from an understanding of purity, order, and chastity—not born from one who is promiscuous, perverted, or not chaste in relation. The man from pure relations is a sign of God, and Prophet Muhammed was the purest of people, born from pure relations from the time of Adam to his parents time, as he claims, so he is a sign of

God and is mentioned in the Quran. The Prophet then married his cousin Khadija and other cousins, including his first cousin from his paternal aunt. The Prophet also married his daughters to cousins, since cousin marriage is obligatory on all Muslims as it is commanded by the Quran in verse (33:50).

Muhammed is chapter forty-seven. Forty is four (awareness) multiplied by ten (perfect giving) plus seven (knowledge or wisdom). So the overall meaning is to grow in knowledge or wisdom, which is apparent in bringing children from pure relations so that they can appreciate the purity of God and also believe in God. The children of pure cousin relations, such as Prophet Muhammed (pbuh) are born from similar parents, and the joining of similar parents is purity, which is the sign of God. Whereas a child born to strangers comes from the joining of different people, making it impure. These children cannot comprehend the existence of the pure God, and so they are born without knowledge of God and with knowledge of sex.

THE CONQUEST

The conquest is a sign of God, and it means an overwhelming power to take control of a distant land. This power is a sign of the existence of the greater power of God. The conquest is chapter forty-eight; forty equals four (awareness) multiplied by ten (perfect giving) plus eight (five and three; five meaning giving and three harm), so the overall meaning is the giving of harm, such as what is done in the wars of a conquest.

THE ROOMS

The rooms is where people come together for intimate relations so as not to be shamed, but since touching is impure in Islam, rooms hide this impurity to proclaim a purity that is a sign of God. The rooms is chapter forty-nine, which means the missing awareness, which is what rooms do.

THE UPSTANDING

The upstanding is a sign of God, since anything good out of the ordinary can remain, prove that goodness exists, and be a sign of God's existence. All things precious, priceless, of high quality, rare, fine, perfect, very good, or outstanding in their fields are upstanding and are thus a sign of God. The upstanding is chapter fifty of the Quran, which overall means 'very good giving'.

THE WINDS

The rain is mercy, and it is important for the growth of plants and the life of animals and humans. Winds come before or accompany the rain as a foretelling of the rain. This makes the winds a reassurance of good things to come or happen, and so it's a sign of God, since God is good. The winds is chapter fifty-one of the Quran. This means fifty is five multiplied by ten (perfect giving) plus one, which means important. The overall meaning is the importance of giving, and this is the description of the winds as they give important news of the coming of rain.

MOUNTAIN OF TOR

The Mount of Tor, also known as Mount Sinai, is where the prophet Moses spoke to God and where Moses is said to have received the commandments. Mountains are a sign of God due to their great sizes, and their grandness is a sign of God. God elevates the mountains towards the sky, making them pure. The mountain of Tor is chapter fifty-two of the Quran. The fifty is five multiplied by ten (perfect giving) plus two, which is union. The overall meaning is the giving of union, which is the description of the mountains, which are unions of smaller rocks.

THE STARS

The stars are the small lights in the dark night sky. The night is a time of deprivation since it is a time when God physically prohibits people from His ownership of fields, rivers, etc. by making people sleep and making it dark. This is to establish that God has a sense of self and ownership, which is called kingship. The stars that are scattered in the sky with no design means little giving, since the stars are not designed sensibly. This strictness in deprivation is to say that the world has an owner, which is God. For this reason, the stars are a sign of God in Islam and stars are a symbol for the kingship of God.

THE MOON

The night is a time of deprivation to establish ownership of God. God has a sense of self and gives as He wishes and refuses as He wishes. However, God created the moon in the night sky as a round light-reflecting object. This is to say that there is an exception to the deprivation since God gives light through the moon. The moon is round, and the round shape is a bent line where its ends meet. A straight line symbolises giving and getting since it's the shortest distance between two points. A round line means a problem that cannot be solved, and so the round shape symbolises need. The light of the moon is giving in times of need, such as in charity, and that is beauty in the world. The appreciation of giving in the symbol of the moon is to say that it is a sign of the goodness in the world and so it is a sign of the good God. The moon is chapter fifty-four in the Quran, because fifty is equal to five multiplied by ten (perfect giving) plus four (awareness or wisdom), and so the overall meaning is the wisdom of giving and that is the meaning of the moon. Prophet Muhammed (pbuh) split the moon as a sign of generosity by dividing it into two parts.

THE COMPASSIONATE

The compassionate is the one who considers benefit as more important than warding off harm and following guidelines. The mercy in the spirit of the law and not following the letter of the law is the meaning of the compassionate. This importance of giving, even in breaking the law, is a kind of mercy, and it is exemplified in the Quran by the story of the Green Man, who tore a hole in the boat so it would not be taken by the king mistakenly to be theirs due to its beauty. He also killed a child to not grow oppressive to pious parents and built a wall to hide treasure from unwelcoming people. The Green Man explained to Prophet Moses his strange doings of going against the law, which were inspired by God's compassion.

Compassion is a sign of God since people go against the established law seeking mercy and goodness, and this keenness towards good things is a sign of the existence of the good God. The compassionate is chapter fifty-five in the Quran, since fifty is five (giving) multiplied by ten (perfect giving), plus another five, giving an overall meaning of the importance of giving.

THE FALLEN

The fallen means what happened or came to exist. This is to say that things happen for real and that there is truth in the world. The past of the world, the history of things that happened, and the shadow of things all show that they physically exist to the point of casting shadows. This truth to the world is a sign of the truth of the existence of God. The fallen is chapter fifty-six, and fifty is five multiplied by ten (perfect giving), plus six, which is two multiplied by three (much harm). The fallen is chapter fifty-six since when things literally fall, they break, and that is harm.

THE IRON

The iron is chapter fifty-seven of the Quran. Fifty is five (emphasis on giving) multiplied by ten (perfect giving), plus seven. Seven is three (harm) plus four (awareness). So the overall meaning of the number fifty-seven is giving, which avoids harm, and since iron is used to shield, ward off harm, or preserve valuables, this keenness to use iron makes it a sign of the good God. Iron strength also shows the power of God's creation.

THE DEBATE

The debate is to discuss a certain point to discover what is right and beneficial, seeking the best. The Quran considers debating a sign of God, since it is seeing what is best and good, thus making it a sign of the good God. The debate is chapter fifty-eight, which is five (giving or emphasis) multiplied by ten (perfect giving) and five and three, is eight. The total meaning is the giving that is harmful. Debates can get pretty heated and it's similar to harm.

THE GATHERING

The gathering of people is good since humans are creatures of goodness and spirit. This makes gatherings a sign of the good God. The gathering is chapter fifty-nine;

fifty is equal to five multiplied by ten (perfect giving) plus nine (shortcoming). When the masses gather, there comes the need to divide resources, so people get less.

THE TESTED

People test things, and this state of examining to find out what is best or what is good is an eagerness towards good things, which is a sign of the good God. The tested is chapter sixty which is six (much harm) multiplied by ten (perfect giving), so testing usually gives strength to what is being tested if it can withstand it. This is like shaking a table severely to check if it's stable.

THE LINE

It takes a lot of effort to put things in a line; some need to be brought near and others need to be put far, and this process is an eagerness to do good, making it a sign of the good God. The line is chapter sixty-one of the Quran. Sixty is six (harm) multiplied by ten (perfect giving) plus one (importance), so the overall meaning of sixty-one means all the effort to put things in line.

FRIDAY

Friday is the sixth day of the week, if the week is considered to start with Sunday and ends with Saturday, like in Arabia. Six means too much harm. The day is half-light (daytime) and half-darkness (night), and that is a joining of two different lights, so it's an impurity.

Since Muslims believe in a pure one God, they consider the day impure and rather celebrate purity on Friday by praying on the sixth day to say that the impurity has been recognised and harm can be avoided. The sixth day also means, that the union of the different day and night, is to the meaning of the number six, meaning harmful. Friday is the sixty-second chapter of the Quran. Sixty is six (much harm) multiplied by ten (perfect giving) plus two (union), and so Friday is the sixty second chapter since sixty-two symbolises harmful union, to say the union of the day and night is harmful and impure.

On Friday, the Prophet Muhammed (pbuh) recommended reading the chapter of the cave of the Quran because Friday is the sixth day and six symbolises harm, and people hide in caves when there is harm or to escape danger. Prophet Muhammed (pbuh) forbade fasting on Friday as a standalone day in Islam, as Friday symbolises purity and is much loved in Islam, and since God is pure, it is considered a day of celebration. The Day of Judgement will be on a Friday. Friday in Arabic is *Juammah* (which literally means 'gathering' or 'assembly'), as people gather when there is harm or danger. In English, it is possible that it is from 'free day', as the sixth day represents harm and so there's a need for rest and becoming free from work. Prophet Muhammed (pbuh) instead recommended fasting Monday and Thursday, since Monday is the second day and so it means couple or mating, making it impure, and Thursday is the fifth day, which is three plus two, meaning the harm of joining, so it's impure. That is why Muslims fast on these days.

THE HYPOCRITES

The hypocrites are people who claim to be Muslim, but harbour disbelief in their hearts. They claim Islam to gain benefits of this world, but they are not sincere towards God. The Quran says such people will be in hellfire. God counts the existence of hypocrites as a sign of God. Even disbelievers lying to become believers is a sign of the greatness of the religion and the existence of God. The hypocrites is chapter sixty-three chapter of the Quran; sixty is equal to six (too much harm) multiplied by ten (perfect giving), plus three (harm), so the total meaning of sixty-three is the giving of too much harm, which is the end of hypocrisy.

THE IGNORED

The ignored is the sixty-fourth chapter of the Quran. Sixty-four is six (too much harm) multiplied by ten (perfect giving), plus four (awareness), so the total meaning is to be aware that harm will happen. When you ignore something, then something wrong happens. The fact that people can sometimes ignore things and nothing bad happens, is counted by the Quran as a sign of the existence of God. Prophet Muhammed (pbuh) said, 'Mention God until people say crazy.' Religion and the mention of God give trust, reliance, and hope that are beyond normal, so that people can become reckless and be mistaken for being insane.

THE DIVORCE

When a relationship loses its benefits and is no longer good, or there is harm or wrong associated with it, it ends in divorce. Divorce is counted as a sign of God in the Quran since it is purity, as there are no longer sexual relations. Divorce is the sixty-fifth chapter of the Quran. Sixty-five is equal to six (too much harm) multiplied by ten (perfect giving) plus five, which is giving or emphasis. The total meaning is that when there is too much harm in giving, divorce happens.

THE FORBIDDING

The forbidding is chapter sixty-six of the Quran. Sixty-six is equal to six (double harm) multiplied by ten (perfect giving). This number, therefore, means that there is too much harm. God made forbidden food, which include alcohol and dirty animals such as pigs, but He allows us to eat clean animals and drink pure drinks, such as water, milk and fruit juice. They have been forbidden to preserve life which is good, and thus forbidding evil is a sign of God.

THE KINGSHIP

Kingship is the sixty-seventh chapter of the Quran. The number means kingship since seven means wisdom and sixty is six (too much harm) multiplied by ten (perfect giving). So, the total meaning is royalty for they are those who are wise and can punish with great harm. Kingship is about identity and ownership, and it is a sign of God since God has a self and a sense of ownership, and God is also the owner of humans and the world. When God is worshipped or called in prayer, He knows it, and when someone or something other than Him is worshipped or called in prayer, He is aware it is not for Him. Therefore, the existence of royalty in the world is a sign of the existence of God and proof of His Kingship.

THE PEN

The pen is the tool of writing, and people use it to record information, to aid understanding and memorisations and to return to knowledge if they forget or become confused. The pen is a sign of God, according to the Quran, since the existence of tools of knowledge is a sign of the existence of the all- knowledgeable God. The pen is number sixty-eight. Sixty-eight is equal to six (too much harm) multiplied by ten (perfect giving) plus eight, so the overall meaning of sixty-eight is the ability to emphasise giving harm. This is the description of the pen, which is that it gives emphasis to or confirms the state of harm, which means forgetfulness.

THE HAPPENING

The happening is the inevitable events. In this world, there are predictable events, such as fire burning and clouds bringing rain. These are signs of the certain existence of God. The happening is the sixty-ninth chapter of Quran. Sixty-nine is equal to is six (too much harm) multiplied by ten (perfect giving) plus nine (shortcoming). This makes the overall meaning of sixty-nine as an awareness of giving something to come or the ability to know the future and avoid harm.

THE ASCENSIONS

The ascension is chapter seventy in the Quran. The seventy is seven multiplied by ten, and seven is six plus one. The meaning of six is too much harm, one means importance, and ten means perfect giving, so the overall meaning of seventy is to be lifted high or elevated, which comes with much harm or pain, such as the climbing of a high mountain.

The birds fly high in the sky; the mountain peaks are high, and this ease of height is a sign of the existence of the powerful God. The Quran says that even angels and spirits ascend to the heavens, and the Prophet Muhammed (pbuh) said, 'When human spirits ascend to God during the night sleep, if they reach the throne the person will get true dreams.' The Prophet Muhammed (pbuh) ascended to God after the night journey to

Jerusalem with the angel, and his blessed body was carried in a heavenly winged mule called *burag*.

NOAH

Noah is the prophet who was saved in the ark with the pairs of animals after God flooded the earth, killing off the unbelievers. Noah is chapter seventy-one of the Quran. Seventy-one is equal to seventy, which means ascensions or elevation, plus one which means important or essential, thus the overall meaning is the importance of elevation, which was the hope of Noah, who needed to be above water to be saved. Noah took care of the animals, and this kindness is also a sign of the good God.

THE SPIRITS

The spirits is the seventy-second chapter of the Quran. The spirits are called *the jinn* in Arabic, and they are gentle creatures that cannot be seen but can see the human world. God counts the spirits as a sign of God since they are gentle and are not made of hard material. God is not a physical entity in Islam, so it is not a surprise that He creates gentle or light creatures, such as *jinn*. The spirits are chapter seventy- two. Seventy means elevation and two means union or creatures, so the overall meaning is the creatures who elevate, which means the spirits since they are light creatures. The jinn also like to fly into the heavens to hear the angels talking of the future and later come and whisper it to psychics, but the Quran says shooting stars are used to deter them from doing that.

THE COMPANION

The companion is the seventy-three chapter of the Quran. Seventy is seven (wisdom and knowledge) multiplied by ten (perfect giving) plus three, which is the addition of two and one; two means union or relationship, and one means important. The overall meaning of seventy-three is the relationship that is important, and this is companionship or friendship. Having company has many benefits; it enriches bonds of attachment, and it can also be there when you are in need. Therefore, companionship is a sign of God, who took the prophets such as Abraham (as) as *Khalil*, or intimate friend.

THE COVERED

To take cover from harm is a defence that protects, and it is a sign of the good God. The covered is chapter seventy- four of the Quran. Seventy is seven (wisdom or knowledge) multiplied by ten (perfect giving) plus four, which is awareness, so the overall meaning is the knowledge of awareness, since in covering, there is no longer the ability to know what is hidden.

JUDGEMENT DAY

Judgement Day is the seventy-fifth chapter of the Quran. Seventy is seven (wisdom) multiplied by ten (perfect giving) plus five, which is to give emphasis, so the overall meaning is giving wisdom, which is what judgement requires. Judgement is to punish wrongdoings and award good deeds, and this is a sign of the good God since it encourages good behaviour and discourages wrongdoings. After death, all people will be raised and be judged by God, and then they'll be sent to eternal bliss if they worshipped God or to eternal hellfire if they were disobedient unbelievers.

THE HUMAN

The human is a sentient being made of kindness, spirit, and understanding if complained to. The human is chapter seventy-six, and seventy means understanding and six means wrong; thus, the human is known to slip and do wrong. The Prophet Muhammed (pbuh) said, 'All sons of Adam do wrong but the best are those who repent to God.'

The Prophet Muhammed (pbuh) said, 'God created Adam in His image,' that is to say that the human is created in the plan of purity. This purity also allows the human to know, appreciate, and worship God as the Quran says, 'God created humans and spirits only to worship God.'

THE MESSAGES

The fact that humans have received messages from God through prophets is a sign of God's existence. The messages is chapter seventy-seven of the holy Quran. Seventy is seven (wisdom or knowledge) multiplied by ten plus seven, and this gives the meaning of seventy seven being the emphasis of knowledge, and that is the meaning of messages.

THE ANNOUNCEMENT

The announcement of things to have happened, or in other words, the news, is to confirm new happenings in the world. The new events announced means that God is still alive and continues to create. The announcement is chapter seventy-eight, and that is equal to seventy (giving of knowledge) plus eight, which is seven (knowledge) plus one (important), so the overall meaning is the important knowledge, and that is what is usually announced.

THE PLUCKING

Plucking is finding a specific thing and pulling on it. In this chapter, the Quran describes the removal of the spirits of the unbelievers at the time of death in a plucking motion. Plucking is specific and certain, and it is the opposite of confusion, such as the plucking of the feathers of a bird in preparation for cooking or the plucking of underarm hair to gain purity in Islam. The plucking is chapter seventy-nine. Seven means knowledge, ten means perfect giving, and nine means shortcoming, so the total meaning of seventy-nine is the knowledge to create a shortcoming or for something to be missing, which is the thing that is plucked. This specific action shows focus and knowledge, which are signs of God.

THE FROWN

God counts frowning at error as a refusal to wrong and a want of good, and since God is good and without error, He doesn't like wrong, so frowning is a sign of God. The frown is chapter eighty of the Quran. Eighty is equal to eight multiplied by ten. Ten is perfect giving, and eight is five plus three; five means giving and three means harm, so the overall meaning is what gives harm, which is why people frown.

THE DARKNESS

The dark hides things revealed by light. Likewise, God exists but is not seen due to the veil of ego and sin. God says in the Quran, 'They are from God veiled' and 'God is nearer to people than their jugular veins.' The darkness is chapter eighty-one, in the Quran. Eighty is eight (comfort) multiplied by ten (perfect giving). Thus, eighty-one is what gives the most form of comfort, and that is because in the dark, people are scared and in the most need of comfort.

THE CREATING

The creating is chapter eighty-two of the Quran. Eighty is comfort giving, and two is union or creating. God is still continuing to create. He still creates rain to allow plants to grow and animals to give birth, because after the initial creation of the world, He still creates. This gives comfort, as we know that there will be fresh water tomorrow and harvest next year to allow people to be comfortable, which will cause them to live. Water came out of the hand of the Prophet Muhammed (pbuh) as a miracle, and this is a sign that God is still powerful without becoming tired.

THE HEEDLESS

Heedlessness is a state of lack of awareness, and that usually happens from a lack of stimuli, so it is a state of purity. God is so pure and considers touching impure, so there are some people who have no awareness. Thus, heedless people are a sign of God. The heedless is chapter eighty-three. Eighty is comfort and three is harm, so overall, it means those who are too comfortable even when there is harm, which is heedless people.

THE SPLITTING

The splitting is chapter eighty-four of the Quran. Eighty is the number for comfort, and four is three plus one, which means what makes people want comfort from much harm which is symbolised by three and the meaning of the number one. God is so pure that He makes splits happen on the earth, cracks on wood, or even the disintegration of little particles of the dead. All this dividing is because God is so pure, and it is the opposite of joining, so splitting things is pure. Prophet Muhammed (pbuh) split the moon as a miracle to give signs of purity that establish the existence of God, who is whole in purity and holy.

THE TOWERS

The towers is chapter eighty-five of the Quran. Eighty means comfort, and five is giving, so the overall meaning is giving comfort. The towers are highly elevated houses, and houses are buildings for rest from work. So houses built towards the sky, which is also a symbol of comfort, mean extra comfort. This state of comfort is a sign of the existence of a good God. In Medina, the Prophet Muhammed (pbuh) lived with the natives of Medina who lived in more than two-story buildings, living on the top floor.

THE SHOOTING STAR

The night sky in its darkness when people are asleep is a deprivation to establish God's ownership. The stars, which produce light, are not arranged in design that give sense, is to say even little is not given, since little light of stars means not giving much. The shooting star is such an extra protective device to make sure that people who are not getting anything are defended. Thus, protecting valuable ownership is a sign of God, and there are some important things such as God. The shooting star is chapter eighty-six. Eighty means comfort or protection, and six means too much harm, so the overall meaning is what protects and can give harm to those who try to steal.

THE HEIGHT

The height is in things like the mountains, stars, or the sky, and all these raised things are a sign of God, who is high in station to His devout believers. God in Islam does not occupy a place even though He has a throne above the seventh heaven. The height is chapter eighty-seven of the Quran. Eighty means comfort, and seven is wisdom, so the elevation and height is usually a safe and comfortable place. For instance, milk was traditionally raised high from cats.

THE FAINTING

The fainting is chapter eighty-eight of the Quran. Eight is comfort and the double use of eight means too much comfort, which is what people who faint need, because they faint from overwhelming harm. Fainting is a defence mechanism, to protect them from being harmed so, it's a form of comfort from harm. God counts failing to not feel harm as a sign of God, as He does not like harm since He is perfect and good. It is said some early Muslims have surgery, such as amputations, during prayer, as they will not feel the pain because they are concentrated in prayer. Perhaps this is an early understanding of anaesthetics in medicine, as fainting is a natural anaesthesia.

THE DAWN

The dawn is the early morning when the sunrays start to appear. The dawn is chapter eighty-nine of the holy Quran. Eighty means comfort, and nine means shortcoming. This means the early morning is a time of comfort after a dangerous night. The early morning is a sign of God since it's the early giving of light, and the beginning of the world comes from God, so dawn is a time that reminds you of God. Muslims perform their first prayer of the day during this time.

THE LAND

The land is made of vast earth, and earth symbolises contentment. This is because the earth depresses when it is stepped on and leaves a mark. Therefore, in Arabic, it is called *bar*, meaning 'obedient', and *ardd*, meaning 'contentment'. The existence of large lands is a sign that there is much contentment in existence, and this is a sign of the good God. The land is chapter ninety, and that is nine (shortcoming) multiplied by ten (perfect giving). This is the number that corresponds to the land, since the earth is depressed when people step on it.

THE SUN

The sun is the largest and hottest object in the sky. It gives rays that touch people, and since touch is impure, it is impure. However, since it moves in the sky and isn't touched for long, it is a sign of purity and a sign of God.

The symbol of purity in the sun meant that people who loved chastity worshipped the sun as god. Abraham, in his early years, thought that the sun was God, but after it set, he considered it as a shortcoming, and so he accepted that the sun wasn't God. The people of Sheba worshipped the sun until King Solomon, who was a prophet of God, was sent to them and caused them to stop worshipping the sun and worship the true God instead. The Prophet Muhammed (pbuh) was said to have been shaded by a cloud in his travels to cover him from the sun's rays in Arabia, and this was one of his miracles. The sun is chapter nighty-one. It's equal to nine (shortcoming) multiplied by ten (great giving) plus one (important). The overall meaning of ninety-one is what is important to be shortcoming or missing, meaning the absence of sunrays as the sun moves across the sky. The sun touches people with its rays, and that is an essential shortcoming since it reminds us of promiscuity.

THE NIGHT

The night is the time of darkness, when people go to sleep and are deprived of the world. This deprivation establishes ownership of God and since God has a sense of self and ownership, He can give or not give as He pleases. Therefore, the night is a sign of God. The night is chapter ninety-two of the Quran. Ninety is nine (shortcoming) multiplied by ten, plus two, which is union or creation. Therefore, the night is a time when there is an inability to see creation.

THE MORNING

The bright morning sun, when things are clear, is a time of lucidity when all things are known. Thus, this clarity is a sign of purity since things can be separated and distinguished, showing a sign of the pure God. The morning is chapter ninety-three of the Quran. Ninety is nine (shortcoming) multiplied by ten (perfect giving), plus three, which is harm. Shortcoming describes the morning since it's early in the day, and harm describes it because of the shining of the sun.

THE EXPLANATION

The Quran lists the explanation as a sign of God. This is because, as people explain the reasons for things, God is the explanation for the existence of this world. The explanation is chapter ninety-four of the Quran. Ninety is nine (shortcoming) multiplied by tens plus four, which is awareness or knowledge. So the overall meaning is the knowledge that is missing, and this is a description of what explanation is, as it provides the knowledge of what people didn't know before. The Hadith or Sunnah, which are what Prophet Muhammed (pbuh) said or did, explain everything about the religion of Islam.

FIGS

Figs are small, round fruits that grow on trees. Trees symbolise need, since unlike animals, they do not have the ability to go to water and thus must be watered where they are. The fig is a tree that is more blatant about desiring and having needs. The fig has many seeds, making it coarse in the middle, which causes it to need water, and thus it should be watered. The figs are usually eaten dry, and the dry seedy core is like sand (dry) as if to say they must be given water. The fig is a sign of God, since only if there was a great God of giving and good would there be such frank asking to be given in the world. The Quran has figs as chapter ninety-five. It's equal to nine, which is shortcoming multiplied by ten plus, and five, which is giving, and so the description of figs is that they are missing water and they must be watered.

THE HANGED

When things are dropped, they fall to a lower level or to the ground and may break. The larger they are, the quicker they fall, and this is, of course, due to gravity. But God created it like this so that it would abase physical matter since it is usually created by the joining of smaller touching particles which is impure and so the larger the more impure and the more they fall. This falling of the large objects because they are more impure, is a sign of the existence of the pure God. This means that to protect things, and to keep them elevated, they have to be hanged. Therefore, to hang things is a sign of God. The hanged is chapter ninety-six of the holy Quran. Ninety-six is nine (shortcoming) times ten plus six (too much harm), so the overall meaning is that if things are not hung, they drop and break.

THE ALLOTTED

The allotted is the portion of sustenance God gives to every creation. God measures this allotted portion, so He gives much to some and others, He gives less. God has known this since the beginning of time and it is all portioned out to wisdom. Part of the belief in Islam is that, Muslims should accept the allotted portion God gives, be it little or much. God gives each person what is needed and may give more to others but God allots what a person requires. For example, rain drops in sizes that don't break the leaves of the plants, amounts of water that do not clog the earth, and in purity so as not to poison or kill the plant. This is allotment, predestination, or fate. It is meant to be like this, as it is optimal and for the best. To accept this in the world and accept God's allottment to his creation is wisdom and is part of the belief in Islam. The allotted is chapter ninety-seven. Ninety-seven is ten (perfection) multiplied by nine (shortcoming), plus seven (wisdom). Therefore, the total meaning is the giving of shortcomings is in wisdom. For instance, people seek and sometimes find meaning in their misfortunes.

THE PROOF

In the world, people usually need proof before taking important decisions, such as a judge giving capital punishment to a criminal or a doctor giving dangerous drugs to a patient. This existence of the idea of proof is a sign of the existence of God, who has all the proof in the world. The proof is chapter ninety-eight of the holy Quran. Ninety-eight is nine times ten, and nine means shortcoming or missing, and eight means comfort, so the overall meaning is to find comfort of proof before something harmful that creates shortcomings is allowed to happen.

THE EARTHQUAKE

The earthquake is the violent movement of the earth, and it is chapter ninety-nine. Nine is shortcoming, and people move away from what causes shortcomings to safety. The emphasis of the number nine is to express the movement, which is the description of an earthquake. The earth is a sign of contentment since it depresses as something steps on it as if being obedient. The earthquake shakes the earth, and this emphasises contentment, or the existence of perfection. Therefore, earthquakes are a sign of the perfect God.

THE HORSES

The horses is chapter one hundred of the holy Quran. One hundred is ten tens, and ten is the perfect giving, making ten twice perfection. Horses are beautiful animals which represent warding off of harm and this is usually done to the most perfect things. This sign of beautiful animals such as horses is a sign of the existence of what is perfect, such as the existence of the perfect God. The God of Islam is the most perfect God of all religions; He is the true God, and so He created horses and spoke about horses in the Quran.

THE BANG

The bang is another name for the last hour in the Quran. The bang is usually another word for order because people bang metals or drums to restore order or to bring attention so that one can perform a certain deed. This call to order, according to the Quran, is a sign of God, who is good and the lord of order and intelligent design. The bang is chapter one hundred and one, where a hundred is perfection and one is important or top, so the overall meaning is to ensure important perfection, which means to call to order with a bang.

THE GREED

The greed in the world is a sign of the existence of a great God because of this internal desire for more comes from knowledge that it can be fulfilled by what God has created. The greed is chapter one hundred and two, where a hundred represents perfection and two means union or increase, so the overall meaning is to desire more of what is perfect, which is greed.

THE AFTERNOON

The afternoon is the time when the sun starts to disappear and the weather becomes dark and starts to cool. The sun's ray touch the skin, so it's impure; however, it is moved across the sky to prevent this touch, so it signifies purity. The afternoon, when the sun's rays are weak, is a time of purity that proves the existence of the pure God. The afternoon is chapter one hundred and three. Hundred is perfection, and three is harm, so the overall meaning is danger or harm in the beginning of darkness.

THE WHISPER

The whisper is a sign of God, because sound is produced when two objects meet and touch is impure. However, a low sound, such as a whisper signifies purity. The whisper is therefore a sign of the pure God, Allah, the god of Islam. The whisper is chapter one hundred and four. Hundred is perfection, and four is awareness or knowledge, so the overall meaning is perfect awareness since sometimes people can't hear a whisper. Whisper could also mean what is perfect or good to be aware of since people whisper important or secret information, such as government officials wearing headphones so important information is whispered to them by their team.

THE ELEPHANT

The elephant is an animal that represents a lack of harm, peace, and caution. This desire for peace is a sign of the existence of the good God, Allah. The elephant is chapter one hundred and five. Hundred is perfection, and five is giving, and that is because those who are cautious want to maintain perfection. The elephant is derived from three words: 'ill fan not', because it is not a fan of ill, or not in harm.

QURISH

Qurish is a tribe of the Arabs, and it comes from two words, *gir she,* which means confirms things. This means confirming only what is good. This eagerness towards what is good, is a sign of the existence of the good God. Qurish is chapter one hundred and six of the holy Quran. Hundred is perfection, and six is too much harm, so the overall meaning is desiring perfection in avoiding harm by choosing what is confirmed to be good. Qurish is the tribe of Prophet Muhammed (pbuh), who lived in Mecca, Arabia.

THE CONTAINER

The container is what holds a substance, so the container is its source, and likewise, God is the source of this world, so the container is a reminder and a sign of God. The container is chapter one hundred and seven. Hundred is perfection, and seven is wisdom, so to have containers is novel wisdom. For instance, instead of eating food in our hands, we have a container such as a plate. The word container or plate in Arabic also means food charity and general kindness.

THE MUCH

The world contains billions of creatures, plants, and planets. All this creation is a sign of a grand God. The much is chapter one hundred and eight. A hundred is perfection, and eight is comfort, and because there is much food and enough water, as well as resources in the world, people are comfortable. The much in Arabic is "*kawthar*", which is also the name of a lake on the Day of Judgement owned by Prophet Muhammed (pbuh) and which he will give to Muslim believers to drink.

THE DISBELIEVERS

The unbelievers are those who refuse to believe in God despite the signs, proofs, and evidence, and therefore refuse to worship God and are happy to enter hellfire. No one is forced to believe in Islam, and so God allowing people to be unbelievers is a sign that God is sufficient, independent, and without need of His creation. This makes the existence of unbelievers as a sign of the great God. The disbelievers is chapter one hundred and nine of the Quran. Hundred is perfection, and nine is shortcoming, and because disbelief is a shortcoming from perfection, unbelievers miss out on what is good and perfect, and that is heaven.

THE VICTORY

The victory is when a group overwhelms another group and defeats them in war. The victory Prophet Muhammed (pbuh) had against the unbelievers of Mecca and elsewhere is a sign of the truth of Islam and the existence of God, who gave the believers victory. The victory is chapter one hundred and ten. Hundred is perfection, and ten is perfect giving; therefore, great giving is the giving of victory.

THE ROPE

The rope is usually used to connect one thing to a much stronger thing. The rope is a sign of God as believers try to establish a connection to God in worship. The rope is chapter one hundred, and eleven. Hundred is perfection and eleven equals ten (perfect giving) plus one (important). This is to say that the rope connects to what is important and perfect, since it connects to something greater and perfect.

The Arabs call the mind the tie, to mean that what works to rules that sane people are not free to do as they wish but restricted to what is already known to be right.

THE SINCERITY

The Quran considers the existence of sincerity, including honesty and genuineness, to be a sign of God. For example, being charitable from the heart, is a sign of the good God. Sincerity also means faithfulness, and chastity means keeping sexual relations for marriage only and these support the existence of the pure God. The sincerity is chapter one hundred and twelve. A hundred is perfection, ten is perfect giving, and two is union or relationship. The overall meaning is a relationship that is perfect, like in faithfulness and sincerity.

THE DAYBREAK

The daybreak is the early morning when the sun's rays first start to shine. The Quran uses *falag*, meaning 'split', as it seems like the sky splits up due to the rays. This is as if there is a great problem and the hope of a solution comes, and this hope is a sign of the good God. The daybreak is chapter one hundred and thirteen. Hundred is perfection, ten is perfect giving, and three is harm, so the overall meaning is giving when there is harm. It is said in the desert that extremely dehydrated people are given water in drops as not to cause an imbalance of their electrolytes. Likewise, God gives good to people in degrees by shining the sun in the early morning, before it intensifies midday.

THE PEOPLE

The human is a special creature, and has the image of God, which is the pure plan of the face. This makes the human a creature that understands, appreciates, and practises purity, which allows it to understand the existence of the pure God. The existence of many people (currently, there are more than seven billion people in the world) is a sign of the existence of God. The people is chapter one hundred and fourteen. Hundred means perfection, ten is the perfect giving, and four is awareness or knowledge; thus, the human is a perfect creature created with knowledge of purity, so this number corresponds to the name of the chapter. The chapter of the people is the last chapter of the holy Quran.

EXTRA SIGNS OF GOD MENTIONED IN THE QURAN
THE STRAIGHT PATH (1:6-7)

The straight path is the idea of being serious and direct and it shows a sign of God. The straight path is that God is so perfect and His religion is so serious that He commands and guides us unto a straight path in religion. This is because there are no bends, no contradictions, no injustices, and no offences in the religion of the perfect God of Islam. This means people being straight and serious in life is a sign of God.

PRAYER AND CHARITY (2:3) (9:60)

The fact that God commands us to do good, and detests evil is a sign that He is a true, good God. The fact that people reach God in prayer and give in charity as they come close to the great goodness and purity of God shows that He is a good God. God wants to be reached in prayer as this relationship establishes a good heart in believers. God says in the Quran, 'Prayer prohibits evil and immorality,' and Muslims are commanded to pray at least five times a day.

Land even Plains (2:22)

The land represents responding to something or contentment since it depresses when it is stepped on. God created humans from mud, which is made from earth (response) and water (purity). God says, 'We only created humans and spirits to worship God.' The vast lands that humans step on is a good sign of God.

The Sky (2:22)

The sky is very high, and height usually donates hardship, such as the climbing of a mountain. The sky being further higher than mountains is as if to say the hardship of hardship meaning destroying hardship or no hardship, meaning comfort. Therefore, the sky is blue, which is the colour of comfort or ease. For instance, a wound once it heals, is no longer painful and becomes blue. Caucasians have blue eyes, which are considered beautiful. This is because eyes are pure and not in hardship since they see without touching from a distance, and so are blue meaning comfort. Other senses such as taste a person's food must touch their tongue with the food, however, the eye there is no touching and so blue eyes are considered beautiful, likewise black eyes since black is the colour of absence and there is absent touch in the eyes. Therefore the sky as a symbol of comfort, is a sign of the good God.

Rain (2:22)

The fact that water, which is a pure substance, falls directly from the sky as rain is a sign of the pure God.

Plant Growth (2:22)

Plant growth requires water and earth. Water is a substance without sensation; it has nothing to see, hear, taste, smell, or feel. It is not made up of the joining of two or more substances or creation, so it is pure. The earth is obedient, as it depresses when stepped on, which means contentment. In plant growth, water, which is pure, has to meet earth, which is contentment, to allow life to be created in the form of plants. This criteria can be met only if water meets the earth, and no life can be formed unless it is contented and accepted by the pure God. This is the law of the legitimacy of the Muslim armies, who are fighting lawfully the aggressive unbelievers for the sake of God. Thus, plant growth is a sign of God and an encouragement to worship God in Islam, the pure religion.

Invent a Book like the Quran (2:23)

The Quran challenges unbelievers to bring or create a chapter or a book like it. This is, of course, impossible since the Quran is a book of numbers; the chapters and verses correspond to numbers, and only God can speak like that. The Quran is a book that corresponds to numbers; it is absolute, and there is no other book like it. This means it can only be from God, for none is like Him. God is absolute. He cannot change. He was not born and will not die. And He speaks based on what corresponds to numbers, so no one can lawfully create a speech of numbers like the Quran because no other god exists with God. God does not only speak about creation in the Quran; He also created it for real. So, if someone wants to write a book to challenge the Quran, then they must also have created what they talk about. The fact that it has been more than a thousand and four hundred years since the revelation of the Quran and this challenge has not yet been fulfilled is a sign of the truthfulness of the Quran and the existence of God.

IMPRESSIVE SPEECH (2:204)

The fact that people say beautiful speeches such as parables, poetry, and wise sayings are all signs of the existence of the wise God. Prophet Muhammed (pbuh) said, 'Some speeches are like magic.'

FIRE (36:80)

Fire is created by touch and friction. When two objects are rubbed together, fire is created that destroys them. Since touching is impure and fire limits touching, fire is therefore a sign of purity in the world, and this is a sign of the existence of the pure God. Since God is completely pure, He has an eternal fire where the unbelievers who do not believe in the purity of God are tortured forever to make them recognise God's purity.

Fire is Fuelled by People and Stones (2:24)

Fire is pure. When sticks are rubbed together, they generate heat and fire to destroy this impure touch, which means that the eternal hellfire is evidence that God is pure. Therefore, burning the unbelievers who refuse God and commit evil and sin is a form of cleansing. God fuelled the hellfire with two elements of touching and joining: stones and humans. Stones are particles of the earth joined together strongly, and humans have the plan of purity of the face to proclaim purity in the world. Also, since the human is a creature of touch and sexual union, it is perfect fuel for eternal hellfire.

Righteousness (2:25)

The good God, who is perfect and pure, is worshipped by doing good deeds, so people doing good deeds is a sign of the perfect and good God.

Heaven has running rivers (2:25)

The heaven that God promised believers has much water, which is a pure element since God is completely pure and holy. The many rivers and oceans in the world filled with pure water are also signs of God.

Mosquitos (2:26)

A tiny insect, which has a small body, is also pure. It also takes up blood to explain that blood relations of a cousin is pure and acceptable to God.

Life from Nothing (2:28)

People did not exist and God created them to be real. So, this existence of life appearing from nothing is a sign of God.

Seven Heavens (2:29)

The Quran teaches us that there are seven heavens. Seven is equal to five plus two, which is also a smart way of saying ten (the perfect giving), therefore seven usually means wisdom. The heavens or sky is very high up, and height is hard to reach, like the climbing of a mountain. The sky is even higher than mountains so high sky is meaning hardship of hardship, which means destroying of hardship, so it means comfort. Therefore, heavens that symbolise comfort are seven. The heavens are also the home of the wise angels who worship God.

Adam (2:30)

God created Adam, the first human, to be a deputy of God on earth. This position entailed looking after the animals and plants. This caring nature in humans and the kindness people show animals and plants are all signs of the good God.

NAMES (2:31)

Names are usually given based on attributes, and this is the basis of language. The fact that humans can communicate with meaning, emotion, and knowledge is a sign of the existence of an intelligent being, which is God.

DIFFERENT LANGUAGES IN THE WORLD (30:22)

The fact that there are different languages in the world is a sign that the ability of humans to speak isn't an accident, and there is emphasise to the idea of speech that comes in the existence of the different languages. In the Hadith, there is an idea that in paradise there will be angels who praise God in all the different languages.

PATIENCE (2:45)

When there is adversity, it disappears after a while. For example, illness heals, so instead of anger and destruction, people practise patience. This patience is a sign of the good God. People know that usually after harm, something good happens, and this is a sign of God.

PHARAOH (79:24)

Because God is so great, Pharaoh was so amazed by His might, that he stole God's identity and claimed to be God, therefore impersonating the Divine. Pharaoh did this in order to get the respect, glory, and affection people gave to God. His desire to be God, is a sign that God exists; otherwise, he wouldn't want to be something that doesn't exist and risk his reputation.

CHILDREN OF ISRAEL (2:40) (5:20)

Israel is the prophet Jacob, the father of Joseph. It is a tribe of many prophets whom God ordered many times to worship Him. The many prophets and the truthfulness of the message to worship Him are all signs of God.

THE SPLIT SEA (2:50)

The Quran mentions the splitting of the Red Sea by the prophet Moses. Water is pure, and its splitting is an act of purity since touching and joining is an impurity. The splitting of the sea is an addition to purity, and this great purity is a sign of God.

VISION OF GOD (2:55) (75:23)

The utmost proof of God is to actually see Him. There are different situations where people have seen or seek seeing God mentioned in the Quran:
1. By the children of Israel in mockery; (2:55)
2. By Moses after talking to God as an additional honour; (7:143)
3. By Prophet Muhammed (pbuh) during the Ascension to the heavens; (53:11)
4. By the believers on the day of judgement; (75:23)
5. By the believers in heaven; (50:35)

6. By the saints who love God and want to be close to God; (18:28)

CLOUDS (2:57) (2:164)

The clouds shade us and protect us from the sun. The sun sends rays that touch our skin, so it's impure, which implies that the shading from the sun's rays is pure. The clouds as purity are thus a sign of the pure God.

JERUSALEM (2:58)

Jerusalem is west of Persia, and Persia is a human race that represents order and prophecy. The west is where the sun sets, meaning for prophecy to fall or to happen, so Jerusalem represents where dreams or prophecies come to pass. The fact that some dreams come true is a sign of the existence of God, who knows what is to happen and can communicate it to people through dreams and the messages of the prophets. As Jerusalem symbolises true prophecy it is considered holy and a sign of God.

EGYPT (2:61)

Egypt is located in the north of Africa. The African race represents the things essential to life and the body; hence, North Africa corresponds to the upper part of the body, such as the pure human face. The Egyptians who inhabit Egypt are white-skinned, unlike the rest of Africans, who are black in colour. White is the colour of purity, and this is therefore an extra sign of the purity of Egypt. Therefore, Egypt is a sign of the pure God.

ILLITERACY OF THE PROPHET (2:78)

Illiteracy is to be unlearned, meaning you do not know how to write. Despite his illiteracy, Prophet Muhammed (pbuh) was very intelligent, wise, and informed. So, the Quran, a book revealed to an illiterate prophet, is a sign of truth that came from God.

JESUS SON OF MARY (2:87), (3:45) AND (19:16-34)

Jesus was born as a miracle from the Virgin Mary without the touch of a man. This form of purity is a sign of the pure God.

ANGEL GABRIEL (2:98)

Angels are creatures that are intelligent, continuously worship God, do not disobey God's orders, and therefore do not sin. Angels were created from light, and since light gives knowledge of what exists, angels are therefore very knowledgeable. A special angel is Angel Gabriel, from Jabreel (*jeeb-ra-eel*) in Arabic, which means 'will bring harm' or in English Gabriel from 'gap are ill'. Therefore, Gabriel is like the king of angels, who is responsible for bringing the holy books warding off the harm of hellfire. Not wanting harm is an understanding that comes from knowing the beauty of the perfect and good God.

Angel Michael (2:98)

Angel Michael is one of the archangels. Michael means 'not to cause harm', and that is why he is the angel responsible for rain and sustenance so that death will not happen. This idea of maintaining a good life is a sign of the good God.

King Solomon (2:102)

King Solomon was the greatest king that ever existed. He was so powerful that he had command over the jinn (spirits) and the wind. He was a prophet of the Jews too. This great kingship is a reminder of the great Kingship of God and therefore a sign of the existence of God.

Direction of Prayer (2:142-144)

In Islam, prayer is done in a direction towards God's House in Mecca. Just as the heart and mind becomes centred on God. The direction of prayer was changed from Jerusalem to Mecca. This sincerity in prayer is a sign of God being real, as there are physical places in Mecca with signs of purity and God more than in Jerusalem.

Boats on Sea (2:164)

The hope and optimism of seeing wood, which used to be from thirsty trees on a sea full of water is a good omen. This sign is a sign of the good God.

Animals escaping Death (2:164) (and 74:50-51)

Animals like deer fleeing from predators and other animals eagerly eating and drinking are all signs of the desire to live, as life is good and is a sign of the good God.

The Cold (24:43) (21:69) (38:42) (56:44) (78:24)

Friction creates fire, but movement such as the flapping of a hand generates cold, so to be cold is purity and therefore a sign of the existence of God. The Prophet Muhammed (pbuh) prayed this prayer: 'God purify us using cold, water and ice.'

Fast of Ramadan (2:183)

Ramadan is the ninth lunar month. Nine is less than ten (perfect giving), and the moon is the giver of light in the darkness, so it represents the giver known as God. The ninth lunar month means a shortcoming in giving, so Muslims fast in the month of Ramadan to protest and proclaim that God is grand and perfect without any shortcomings. The Quran that commands the fast of Ramadan is thus a sign that it came from a God complete in goodness.

Answered Prayers (2:186)

Many people pray to God, and their prayers are answered, so this is a sign that God exists. People pray to God, especially during emergencies, and many people live where there's danger, so this is anecdotal evidence of the existence of God.

Martyrs (2:190)

All those who fought in the way of God and died give witness to the existence of God. God commands Muslims to be peaceful with others. He does not love the aggressors and prohibits terrorism in the name of God and Islam. However, when it is a lawful war between two groups prepared with arms, it is an honour to be a martyr.

Life after Death in this World (2:243)

In many instances, the Quran claims that God gives life after death. This includes an army (2:243) and Jews mocking God by saying that they will only believe if they see God (2:55-56) and the man revived by the touch of a cow (2:73). Another instance is when God created birds, and their divided bodies, which were put at different mountains, still came together and lived (2:260).

Harvest (2:261)

That one seed brings seven ears, each with a hundred seeds or more. This increase is from a grand God and it is nothing to God, like a 'needle tip taking a drop from the sea'. God still gives, and He is eternally rich.

Loans (2:282)

A person takes a loan when he is in need but returns it to the lender. Likewise, people take from God to live and therefore need to return that life by worshipping and praising God. The word religion in Arabic is *deen* which comes from the word *dayn,* also known as loan. The trust between people in giving and returning God is a sign of goodness in the world, that is a sign of God.

IMAGE OF HUMANS (3:6)

The image of humans is special. It is not of a random design, but there is a design that proves that it was created by God. Our image was designed such that the nose looks like a male and the mouth looks like a female. These two are permanently separated and not allowed to touch, and this is a form of chastity, purity, and honour. Likewise, the Prophet Muhammed (pbuh) said that the act of sexual union is *sadaga*, which means charity or truthfulness, since the union of the male and female genitalia during sexual intercourse is an affirmation of the face, and so it also proves the existence of God. The Prophet Muhammed (pbuh) said God created humans in the image of Himself, which means an image of purity that proclaims the existence of the pure God.

MIRACLES OF THE PROPHETS (3:49)

The miracles of the prophets which were witnessed and recorded by the people in their time, are some of the proofs of their truthfulness as prophets and a sign of the existence of God. Jesus, who in Islam is believed to be only a prophet, healed the ill, the dumb, the lepers, and gave life to the dead. He also created birds from mud and breathed into them, and they became living beings. Abraham also cut birds into pieces and placed them on different mountains, and they came flying down with the power of God. Prophet Muhammed (pbuh) also produced water from his noble hands, split the moon, and fed hundreds of people with little food. All these recorded miracles of the prophets are signs of God.

VICTORS OF GOD (3:52)

Victors of God are people who strongly support God and the prophets, such as the disciples of Jesus and the companions of Prophet Muhammed (pbuh) and saints. Their determination and sincerity in religion is a sign there is truthfulness to God and religion.

DEATH (3:55), (3:185) AND (4:78)

In death, the body disintegrates into smaller particles. This is a sign of purity since it is the opposite of joining and touching, which are impure. At the moment Prophet Muhammed (pbuh) died, he said to the angel of death that he would rather die and return to the company of God. This is because after death, the world is all centred around God, and everything will depend on your relationship with God and your worship. Therefore death is a sign of God and our return to Him in the hereafter.

SWEARING OF THE PROPHETS (3:61)

In the Quran, the Prophet Muhammed (pbuh) was told by God to swear in His name and on behalf of his family that the religion of Islam is the truth of God and that a curse shall befall him and his family if he was a liar. This supports the religion and is a sign of the true existence of God and the truth of the religion of Islam.

PURITY IN THE WORLD (3:67) (4:125)

The pure ideas in the world all point towards the existence of the pure creator—God. This belief in the purity of the world is called *hanafiya,* and it was the religion of Prophet Abraham that Islam is based on.

TRUST (3:75) (2:282)

Trust involves giving people back what is due them, as did the Prophet Muhammed (pbuh) who people before Islam trusted him with their valuables. This shows that there is something greater than the world, and that is God.

THE ISLAMIC RELIGION (3:85)

A religion in which people purify themselves before prayer and also proclaim a perfect God is a sign that it came from a true and pure God.

BATTLE OF BADR (3:123-126)

In the battle of Badr, the Muslim believers won the war even though they were fewer in number. This is because

God sent angels who fought with the believers. This victory in battle is a sign of God.

THE ARAB PROPHET (3:144)

Arabs avoid harm in the desert, and therefore it makes sense to make the royal an Arab prophet—one who preaches to people to help them avoid hellfire. Prophet Muhammed (pbuh), the Arab Prophet who was royal (a lord), is thus a sign of the truthfulness of the message and also a sign of the existence of the true God.

DROWSINESS IN WAR (3:154)

God gave the believers fighting during sleep to keep them safe in times of war. This safety, even during a dangerous war, is a sign of the good God.

ADAM AND EVE (4:1)

God created Eve from the flesh and blood of Adam, and this is a sign of purity, because when they join in holy matrimony, it is the joining of similarity, and that makes it pure. This purity of Adam and Eve is a sign of the purity and existence of God.

INHERITANCE OF FAMILY (4:2) (4:6)

In Islam, life should come from cousin marriage (33:50) and from family. Likewise, in the event of death, ownership should go to the family. This is a form of purity, since the family of the deceased is comforted by the properties. This form of kindness supports the idea of the goodness of God.

Four Wives Maximum (4:3)

In Islam, the maximum number of wives to have is four. Four means awareness since four lines make a square and these corners can be felt. This square is the opposite to a circle that has no corners and cannot be felt since it is smooth. So for a man to have more than four wives, is to mean aware of more body flesh, and this sounds like as if he was in a relationship with a man, and as this is impure it is prohibited in Islam. This pure marriage of four or less wives shows that God is pure, and He exists.

Trade (4:29)

Trade involves exchanging goods of similar value. There is a lot of giving to humans from God, and a lot of rich people and so not everything is charity; some own enough to buy in trade. This shows that good exists, which is proof of God.

Ablution of Earth (4:43)

Ablution of the earth means to wipe the face and hands after touching the earth. This is the hopeful purification, called *tayamum,* and it is done when there is no water to do a water ablution called *wadu*. The earth is considered pure in Islam since it symbolises obedience and giving, and it depresses when it is stepped on. The insistent need to purify yourself before approaching God in prayer, even by doing earthly purification, is proof of the total purity of God and a sign of His existence.

Burning of Skin in Hellfire (4:56)

God burns the skins of disbelievers in hellfire, and once they are burnt, they regenerate new skin to be burned again. The pure God burns the skin, which is impure, as skin is a place of touch so this burning is a form of purifying that proves that the pure God exists.

Greetings (4:86)

The readiness to preserve life and send peace to anyone by greeting people is a sign that there are still good people in the world, and so it is a sign of God. The Islamic greeting is *assalamu alaikum,* which means 'peace be upon you'.

Punishment for Killing Life (4:92-93)

The details about the punishment for killing a person, even by accident, show the strictness of God, who is the giver of life and all good. This law sees life as important and judges anyone who takes it, and this is a sign of the good God.

No Hunting During Pilgrimage (5:32)

In Islam, pilgrims are not allowed to hunt. This prohibition to kill life, is a sign of the goodness associated with the

House of God, which is all proof that this command comes from a pure and good God.

Immigration for God (4:100)

People travel to find places where it is easy to worship God. This is a sign of insisting on worshipping God, and this keenness means God is real.

Prayer of Fear (4:102)

The Quran commands Muslims to take turns praying during times of fear of attack. This keenness for prayer and the fact that, in fear, people turn back to God are all signs of God's existence.

No pointless Chatting and Playing for Adults (4:114) and (23:3)

The fact that people trivialise chatting and playing is a sign that there is something serious in this world, and that is God and religion.

Ablution (5:6)

Muslims are commanded to use water to wash themselves before prayer. This is done so that they can purify themselves. This purity is a sign of the existence of the pure God.

Punishment for Stealing (5:38)

In Islam, the one who steals is punished by cutting off his hand. God, the perfect God, cannot give His divinity to others, so only He is worshipped. Likewise, ownership is sacred and should not be taken without permission. This strictness is to ensure justice and peace between people.

Fine for Swearing by God (5:89)

A Muslim must feed or clothe ten people, free a slave, or fast for three days. If they swear by God but do not fulfil it, or they break a promise in the name of God, then such is the reverence for God in Islam. This reverence for the name of God is a sign of the truthfulness of the religion of Islam.

Prohibition on Gambling (5:90-91)

Nothing is random, and everything is according to God's plan. God is behind the design of the world, and therefore random gains in gambling are not allowed in Islam. Therefore, prohibiting gambling is a sign of accepting the plan and design of God, and this is a sign of the existence of the planner, God.

Feast from Heaven (5:114 -115)

God helps us maintain life by providing us with life and food from heaven. An example is the feast of Jesus and his disciples. Mary, the mother of Jesus, was also said to have been given grapes that were not in season, so this could be from heaven. This keenness for life is a sign of the good God.

Destroyed Nations of the Past (6:6)

God destroyed towns and cities that did not believe in Him, so they disappeared from the face of the earth. The great punishment of God is a sign of the great evidence for God, so rejecting God and good things is a great crime punished by God. The fact that there are no longer nations that did not believe in God after prophets were sent to them is a sign of the true existence of God.

Birds (6:38) (67:19)

Birds represent no touching, and therefore, they are made of feathers that, if touched, is not felt by the bird as feathers block it. Birds fly high in the sky distancing itself as not to be touched. This lack of touch in birds is a sign of purity, and the Quran says birds maintain their flight in the sky to proclaim God's existence. This is because their stationary state in flight means continuity in purity, and only God is whole in purity.

Rewarding of Good and Bad (6:160)

Good behaviour is rewarded ten times, but bad behaviour is counted and punished only once. This is good and is a sign that the religion comes from a God who is truly good and just.

Modesty (7:22) (7:26) (33:59) (24:31)

Adam and Eve covered their modesty quickly with leaves to prevent their exposure in heaven to God, who does not want harm. However, in Islam, there is a command in the Quran to cover shame, which means to be modest in the presence of God. This is the reason why Muslim women cover themselves in public in what is called *hijab*. This covering is a sign of purity as it prohibits the arousal of sexual feelings between people in public. This command to cover up in the Quran is a sign that the religion comes truly from a pure God.

CAMEL FROM STONE (7:73)

Stones imply small joining, so it is pure, and a camel means great giving, so the total meaning is so much purity, which is a sign of God.

SNAKE FROM STICK (7:107)

Snakes represent harm, as they crawl on the earth like a person in pain. Also, for a snake to change into a stick means to stop harm. God gave Moses the miracle of changing a stick into a snake and vice versa to show that God, the reliever of pain, is real and exists.

GRAPES (13:4)

This is a tree that symbolises resisting hardship. It is round and elongated; round means needy since it's a bent line, and elongated means far or distant. So the overall meaning is no longer needed. It tastes like sweet water, which implies that it is nice to get water, and it crawls so that it can reach water, unlike other trees that are stationary. The fact that there are trees that symbolise resisting hardship is a good sign in the world, and that is a sign of the existence of the good God.

Date Palm (13:4)

The date tree symbolises given, which means it has been given water. This is why it is very sweet, as it is happy, so it symbolises gratitude. Being grateful is a sign of the good God.

The Quran in Arabic (13:37)

Arabs try to avoid harm in the desert, and since religion is to avoid hellfire, it is appropriate for the Quran to be in the Arabic language and for the prophet to be an Arab. The fact that God sent His words in Arabic shows that He cares for people to avoid hellfire, and this mercy is a sign that the good God exists.

The Devil (14:22)

God is good and perfect, and the world is good and perfect, that evil cannot come from God but is created by creation, such as the devil who inspires to wrong. This is a sign that God is perfect beyond wrong, and wrong comes only from creation.

Olives (16:11)

Olive is the fruit of a tree that is very oily. It represents the awareness of oneself. This is because oil is a sign of awareness of self, as it slips, meaning as. If being defensive by moving others away from belonging. It is also yellow, the colour of harm, so it's the absence of white (purity and goodness). God created the olive since trees are usually wise with fruits that have meaning for the tree's life. Therefore, God creating the olive signifies the existence of God, who has an awareness of Himself. Jesus is considered to be the Messiah and in Arabic this comes from a word meaning anointed, as he was anointed by olive oil to proclaim his progeny from the kings of the Jews.

FISH (16:14)

Water is pure, and the fish living in this pure water is a sign of the existence of the pure God. Fish represent confirmation since they move around things to confirm they exist, i.e., a shark swimming around its prey. This sureness even in fishes is a sign of the true existence of the certain God.

PEARLS (16:14) (55:22)

Pearls symbolise the ability to not take what is not yours. In Arabic, pearls are *lolo* and *looly* (from the words meaning 'if mine'). It is round, white, and hard; round means need, white means pure or repeat, and hard means strong. The complete meaning is that it will only 'take in hardship'. This symbol of ownership is thus a sign of honesty, and God doesn't share His divinity with creation, so pearls are a sign of the existence of God.

Born Innocent (16:78)

Babies are born ignorant, meaning without knowledge, and their minds do not understand complex things, which is a kind of purity. The ignorance and innocence of babies is thus a sign of the pure God.

Sight (16:78)

Seeing happens from a distance without any form of joining or touch, unlike taste, where food has to touch the tongue to be tasted, or the skin, where it has to be touched before it is felt. This recognition of objects in our surroundings without touching them is a sign of the existence of the pure God.

Hearing (16:78)

Hearing is the detection of sound. Sound is produced when two things touch and knock on each other, and since this is impure and can create fire, God created hearing to detect this touch and stop it. Thus, hearing is pure and a sign of the pure God. Since sound is impure, that is the basis for forbidding music in some schools of thought in Islam.

Armour (16:81)

Knights traditionally wore armour in war to avoid harm and death. This keen desire to live is a sign of the good God. Armour is said to have been invented by the prophet David.

The Spirit (17:85)

The spirit helps one to be aware of other beings than oneself, and also show kindness towards others. For instance, if a goat falls into a well, the other goats do not cry and try to remove it, but if a human falls into the well, other people will come to cry in sadness and try to remove him/her from the well. This attempt to pull out the fallen person is a kindness that only exists in humans. The spirit is indeed good, and that is a sign of the good God.

Moses Spoke to God (20:11-36)

A proof of the existence of God is that Moses spoke to Him. This is recorded in many holy books.

Paths on Earth (20:53)

The fact that there are paths to travel from one place to another is a sign that the world was created by an intelligent being. Therefore, the Quran counts the paths on earth as signs of God.

Creating in Stages (22:5) (23:14)

The ability to create humans or clouds to form rain that take stages is a sign of the insistence to create by overcoming steps. The fact that it requires steps is no deterrent for God to create. This is a sign of the power and intelligence of God's existence.

Rich People (28:76)

The fact that rich people exist is a sign of the richness and power of God. Rich people are a sign of God.

Age of Noah (29:14)

Noah lived for nearly a thousand years, or nine hundred and ninety-five years, to be exact. This long life that people in the past lived is a good sign, since life is good. It is therefore a sign of the good God.

Books (29:48)

There are many books in the world, and they contain much knowledge. People write to remember and to give facts, and this sign of knowledge in the world is a sign of the knowledgeable God.

Tasty Food from Water (13:4)

The fact that from plain water come fruits and foods rich in taste and flavour is a sign of God, since this addition comes from God.

Date Palm divided into Trunk (13:4)

The fact that some trees divide their trunks to give off extra branches and fruits, depicting good and extra giving, is a sign of the good God.

Old age (36:68)

Those that grow old inevitably decrease in strength, as if God is limiting grander to Him alone. Likewise, when something is praised without any mention of God, it is destroyed, this is called the "evil eye" and Muslims are commanded to praise God upon seeing anything beautiful or perfect.

Riding Animals (36:72)

Controlling animals when riding them is also a symbol that signifies the restraining desire in humans. This control is a good sign, and that is a sign of the great God.

Dreams (12:4)

The fact that even after sleep, there are dreams where people sense, see, feel, and are aware of their surroundings is a sign that there will be life after the body dies. Sometimes people's dreams come true, and this is a sign of God, who inspires the future into the hearts of people during their sleep.

Shadows (16:48)

Shadows appear when light hits an object that it can't penetrate, so it gives off a dark shadow. This gives a strong sense of reality—that things are real, and if they can give shadows, then they are hard. This sense of reality is a sign of the true existence of God.

Honey (16:69)

The fact that there is something so sweet is a sign of a good God.

SANITY (47:5)

Sanity is a state of desiring good things and refusing harm from self and others. The fact that the majority of people are sane is a sign of goodness, and that is also a sign of the good God.

FLOWERS (55:12) (56:89)

Flowers are the parts of the plant that grow into fruits and contain male and female parts. The Quran also mentions the flowers of *Rayhan,* which are flowers that give off a beautiful minty smell. The Prophet Muhammed (pbuh) also mentioned that in heaven, the grass will be saffron. Saffron is a special flower where the female part is outside the flower, as if running away in shyness from the male that is inside the flower, so it's pure, and the celestial virgins of paradise will be created from this saffron flower. The purity of flowers and the good smells they give off is a sign of a good and pure God.

SUFFERING (CHAPTER 12)

The chapter of Joseph tells us of the story of his suffering: first he was thrown into a well by his brothers, then he was sold into slavery, then he was accused of rape, and then he was sent to prison. However, he later became a royal in Egypt as his life turned around. This turnaround is a sign of a one true God. This is because many other gods share the power of God, and thus they become weak and can't help, but a one true God has all the power of

God alone and can remove hardship. Joseph said, 'Many gods are better or the one God who is Majestic' (12:39). Therefore in Islam, suffering and hardship are seen as God trying to emphasise to the believers that He is a one God.

HEALING (17:82)

The fact that many people heal after an illness and that God created cures such as honey is a sign that there is a powerful God and demonstrates His goodness. This makes healing and being cured a sign of the good God.

GUILT (90:10)

The fact that people feel guilty when they do something bad is a sign that they were created by a good God who exists.

HUMANS DIFFERENT IN COLOUR (30:22)

God created humans in different shades; some are white, some are yellow, some are brown and others are black. There are some colours that say skin should be pure, like white, which is the colour of the light, so it's purity. Yellow is a colour that symbolises harm. White skin means purity and implies that people should be chaste. Yellow signifies harm so yellow skin says touch is an impurity, and black is the colour of absence meaning absence of sexual touch and so also means purity. Brown is a colour before black so means small giving such as the giving of babies, and since they need to be brought in pure relations brown skin also carried ideas of purity. The human is a pure creature, and God created it in many colours of purity to emphasise that it should be pure and worship a pure God. The purity of the colours of humans is a sign that the creator is pure and exists.

SEX (2:187) (4:43)

The human face has a nose that looks like a male and a mouth that looks like a female, and their permanent separation is a sign of purity that supports the idea that the human came from a pure creator, God. The act of sex, where the male genitalia penetrate the female genitalia, supports the existence of God. This means sex supports the truth of God's existence. Prophet Muhammed (pbuh) said sex is charity since the man gives flesh to the woman and used the word *Sadaga*, which, as well as charity, means to give truth. The first act of sex between virgins further supports the existence of God since it emphasises purity since it is difficult to get the male to join the female.

ISHMAEL (21:85)

Ishmael is faith against odds. Ishmael was born to parents who were strangers, while his brother Isaac was born to parents who were cousins. In cousin parents, the child is born from parents who are similar in blood and flesh, and thus they join in purity. Since creating in purity supports the existence of a pure creator, (God) the child of cousin marriage easily accepts the existence of God. However, in stranger marriages, the joining of two impure individuals doesn't support a pure creator, so they are born as atheists. Now, Ishmael, even though he was born to strangers and was born an atheist, submitted to the God who commanded him to be killed, and he built the house of God in Mecca with his father Abraham. This is faith against all odds, and against his natural creation and inclination, Ishmael believed in God. This is very beautiful and inspiring, so God made Ishmael a prophet. Because Ishmael believed in God even though he was born of impure parents, this confirms the absolute existence of God.

ABOUT THE AUTHOR

Mysa Elsheikh is a Muslim Arab Queen (Um-fugara or Mother of the Poor) from Sudan. Her full name is: Mysa daughter of Mohamed Elgasim son of Elsheikh Almagzoub. Mysa is the 61 direct descendant from Prophet Muhammed (pbuh) on her father's side and number 62 from her mother's side. She is also a descendant of Abdullah ibn Abass (raa), Prophet Muhammed's cousin and great Quran scholar. Mysa learned Arabic and the Quran in Sudan as a child, and she attended her grandfather's Quran School (*khalwa*) with her brother. Mysa once qualified for a high IQ society when she was young, and she did her GCSE Maths and Arabic a year earlier studying for both on her own, and she received A* on both, she also received an A* on Religion Education. Mysa studied Medicine at St George's University of London, she graduated early in the course by leaving in the third year with a diploma in Medical Studies. She left Medicine mainly because she wanted to finish her book Ihsan, and pursue a career in writing Islamic books and calling people to God and Islam. She studied a Medical summer course at Magdalen College University of Oxford. She also studied a year of Psychology and Creative Writing at Bolton University. She also studied two years of Medicine at Ahfad University for Women in Sudan.

Inspired by a dream of Prophet Muhammed (pbuh) in the Christmas holiday of 2003, she was guided to study Sufism (Ihsan) with her paternal uncle, King Sheikh Jaily son of Elsheikh Almagzoub of Albaneya, Sudan. In the summer of 2004 she took a formal pact and became initiated into Sammaniya Sufi Path. Four months later at the age of 19 years old, Mysa has a vision of God walking down Longmead Road, in south London, Britain. In the Vision of God, Mysa saw God, Allah, the God of Islam. She reports seeing an ocean of light, that there was light to her right, and light to her left, and light above her and light below her, and light in front of her and light behind her and even light inside her. The light penetrated everything hard and solid, and it was as if she was drowning in an ocean of light. Before the vision, Mysa was for months begging God to give her His vision, and this was out of her great love for God and in seeking the divine beauty of God. Mysa comes from a family of Sufi (Ihsan) scholars, and her grandfathers and forefathers called Magazeeb of Damer were all Sufi scholars and Saints in Sudan for more than 500 years. Mysa was the favourite granddaughter of the great Sufi saint, King Sheikh Magzoub of Albaneya, Sudan (died 1986). In May 2022 she married her first cousin to fulfil verse (33:50) of the Quran and after another dream of Prophet Muhammed (pbuh), Sheikh Hamza son of Sheikh Awadallah son of Elsheikh Almagzoub. In November 2022 she accepted her first Ihsan (Sufi) Student. Mysa is a famous influencer in Sudan and as of June 2023 she has over 50,000 followers on TikTok alone and many viral videos watched by millions.

Mysa is fortunate to be a descendant of Prophet Muhammed (pbuh) and her Genealogy to Prophet Muhammed (pbuh):

Mysa daughter of Sharif Mohammed Algasim, son of Sharif Magzoub, son of Sharifiya Sakeena, daughter of Sharif Fadul is the son of Sharif Hussain, son of Sharif Ibrahim, son of Sharif Muhammed, son of Sharif Hamad, son of Sharif Muahmmed Zumrawi, son of Sharif Muhammed Ahmed Al Bagir, son of Sharif Mahmoud, son of Sharif Hamad, son of Sharif Abdalkareem, son of Sharif Hassaballah Abu Khuf, son of Sharif Muhammed Almadani, son of Sharif Jabal, son of Sharif Abdullah, son of Sharif Barakat, son of Sharif Gasim, son of Sharif Rattib, son of Sharif Shahwan, son of Sharif Messaya, son of Sharif Taglab, son of Sharif Hober, son of Sharif Zakir, son of Sharif Sirajaldeen, son of Sharif Ja Alnaser, son of Sharif Gais, son of Sharif Shafi, son of Sharif Fayed, son of Sharif Umayra, son of Sharif Umran, son of Sharif Ali Noraldeen Ameel Murij, son of Sharif Hussain, son of Sharif Hassan Alakbar, son of Sharif Ali Albadri, son of Sharif Ibrahim, son of Sharif Muhammed, son of Sharif Abi Baker, son of Sharif Ismael, son of Sharif Umar, son of Sharif Ali, son of Sharif Usman, son of

Sharif Hassan, son of Sharif Muhammed, son of Sharif Mosa, son of Sharif Yahya, son of Sharif Essa, son of Sharif Ali, son of Imam Muhammed Altagi, son of Imam Hassan Alaskari, son of Imam Muhammed Alhadi, son of Imam Muhammed Aljawad, son of Imam Ali Alrida, son of Imam Mosa Alkazim, son of Imam Jafer Alsadig, son of Imam Muhammed Albagir, son of Imam Ali zain Alabdeen, son of Imam Hussain, son of Imam Ali and son of Fatimah daughter of Muhammed (pbuh) the Prophet of Islam.

www.ingramcontent.com/pod-product-compliance
Lightning Source LLC
Chambersburg PA
CBHW072048290426
44110CB00014B/1601